Department of the Environment
Ancient Monuments and Historic Buildings

Tower of London

Greater London

R ALLEN BROWN   MA, D Litt, FSA
Professor of History, University of London, King's College

and

P E CURNOW   BSc, FSA
*Principal Inspector of Ancient Monuments
and Historic Buildings*

LONDON: HER MAJESTY'S STATIONERY OFFICE

Contents

© *Crown copyright 1984*
First published 1984

Printed by HMSO Press, Edinburgh
Dd 718571 C412 2/84 (204954)

ISBN 0 11 671148 5

Illustrations

Acknowledgements

The Department of the Environment wishes to thank Aerofilms for permission to reproduce plate XXVI, the Ashmolean Library for plate XXVI and the British Museum for plate IX. The engravings in plates XII, XXII and XXV are by Nash from Bayley's *History and Antiquities of the Tower of London* (1821). Remaining photographs are Crown copyright from the DoE Photographic Library. Reconstruction illustrations by Terry Ball of the Directorate of Ancient Monuments and Historic Buildings. Much valuable information for the later period was provided by Geoffrey Parnell, working at the Tower on behalf of the Department.

History

Almost from the beginning, at the time of the Norman Conquest, this royal castle in London (then taking the place of Winchester as the principal royal city in the realm) has been known not as London Castle but as the Tower of London, because of the great White Tower which dominated it and still does. The foundation of the castle, however, comes before the building of the great tower within it a decade or so later, and most probably occurred in the very year of the Conquest and as part and parcel of the Norman occupation of London in the winter of 1066. After his victory at Hastings on October 14, the Conqueror made a slow, intimidating and circuitous advance upon London, founding castles as he went, via Dover, Canterbury, Winchester, Wallingford (where he crossed the Thames) and Little Berkhampstead. Here, at a date which must already have been in December, the chief men of the city and many of the surviving English magnates came in to submit to him, and the Norman duke, according to William of Poitiers his biographer, sent an advance party to the city to construct a castle within it and to make preparations for his triumphal entry. Again, the same writer tells us that, after his coronation in Westminster Abbey on Christmas Day 1066, the new king withdrew to Barking 'while certain fortifications were completed in the city against the restlessness of the huge and brutal populace. For he [William] realized that it was of the first importance to overawe the Londoners'. In these events we may properly see both the use of castles by the Normans to impose their rule upon the conquered kingdom and, more particularly, the founding of the future 'Tower of London' together with, in all probability, the other two early Norman castles in the city—Baynard's Castle, in the south-west angle, and the castle of Monfichet to the north of it (near Ludgate Circus).

The new royal castle was at first evidently an enclosure within the south-east angle of the then surviving Roman city walls (cf Porchester) whose existing strength it utilized to east and south as well as the defence and access provided by the Thames (Fig 2). Recent excavations by the Department of the Environment have revealed due south of the White Tower a section of the fourth-century Roman river-wall, including the hitherto unexplained re-entrant which has determined the line of the south curtain of the castle in this area ever since. Earlier excavations in 1964 and 1974–75 had already discovered, respectively north and south-west of the White Tower, early ditches which must represent the first enclosure of the Norman castle within the city walls. The first of these ditches, 8m wide by 3.5m deep, is no longer visible but ran from a point on the eastern Roman city wall just north of the White Tower, in a south-westerly direction to turn south towards the river at a point roughly opposite the present Bloody Tower. The other ditch, which is not quite aligned with the first, may still be seen at the western foot of the later Main Guard Wall, running in a northerly direction

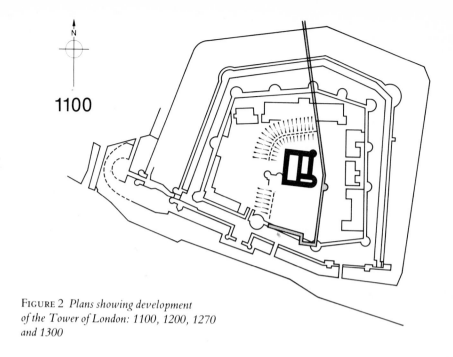

N

1100

FIGURE 2 *Plans showing development of the Tower of London: 1100, 1200, 1270 and 1300*

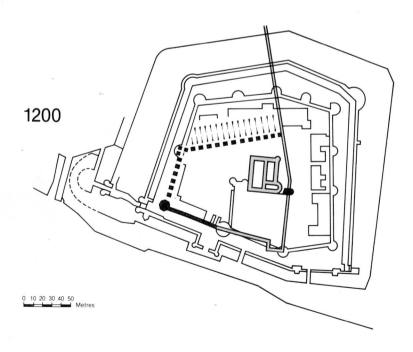

1200

0 10 20 30 40 50
Metres

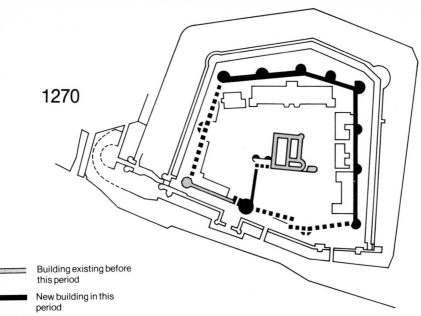

1270

Building existing before
this period

New building in this
period

Conjectural new building
in this period

Outline of present Tower
buildings

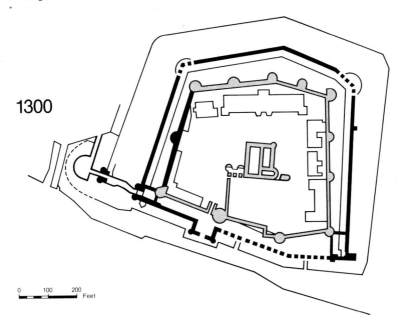

1300

0   100   200
              Feet

from the present Bloody and Wakefield towers (Fig 2).

Inside the enclosure thus formed, doubtless further defended at first by timber palisades to north and west, there must always have been, from as early as possible, accommodation suitable for the warrior king and his court. Nevertheless, within about a decade of the Conquest truly palatial accommodation was provided for the king's majesty in the form of the White Tower (Pl I). Traditionally ascribed to 1078, its exact date is unkown as is the period required to complete it: all that is certain is that it was at least begun in the Conqueror's reign (1066–87) and was building at some time after 1077. The *Textus Roffensis*, which is a register of the cathedral priory of Rochester, explaining the circumstances in which a certain piece of London property came into the possession of the monks there, describes how the gift was first offered when Gundulf, bishop of Rochester, was lodging in the house of the donor, Eadmer Anhaende, a London burgess, and 'while the same Gundulf, by command of king William the Great, was in charge of the work of the great tower of London'. Gundulf, we know, was a man of parts, a monk from Bec in Normandy, a protegé of archbishop Lanfranc, brought over to England by him and subsequently appointed to the bishopric of Rochester in 1077. In relation to building, also, Gundulf was evidently something more than a mere administrator or, in the language

PLATE I (OPPOSITE) *The White Tower, showing the south-east apsidal projection, the north-east cylindrical turret and the entrance at the first-floor level on the south (The Wardrobe Tower and the line of the Roman Wall are in the foreground)*

of a later age, 'clerk of works', for the same *Textus Roffensis*. in describing how he subsequently came to build Rochester castle for William Rufus, writes of him as 'very competent and skilful at building in stone'. This bishop also, like a true Norman prelate, rebuilt the cathedral church at Rochester, built new claustral buildings for his monks

PLATE II *The Chapel of St John in the White Tower*

there, and founded and built the nunnery at Malling.

Although Gundulf's great tower will be fully described hereafter (pp 59–68), it is fitting to pause here a moment to emphasize its deliberate majesty. Architecturally what the French call the *pièce maîtresse* of the whole building, it was at one and the same time the military strong-point of the castle and housed the grandest residential accommodation including that for the king himself.

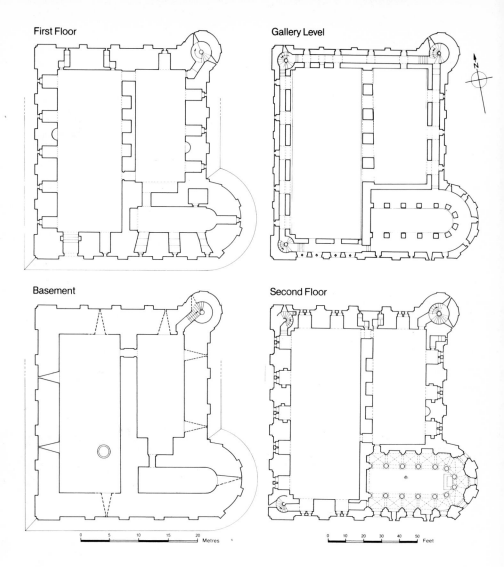

First Floor

Gallery Level

Basement

Second Floor

0 5 10 15 20 Metres

0 10 20 30 40 50 Feet

It was, in contemporary terms, the *don-jon*—a medieval Latin term derived from the Latin *dominium* signifying lordship. As such it is one of the largest donjons of the great-tower type surviving in Europe, a fitting habitation for him who had become one of the most powerful princes in Christendom. Its internal splendours now are masked by the Armouries it contains, but still in the chapel of St John (Pl II), perhaps, one can get as close to William the Conqueror and his God of Battles as anywhere in England or Normandy. *Arx palatina* William fitz Stephen called it in the next century, and a fortified palace it was in an age when the word palace was used sparingly, and exclusively for regal majesty. Technically, in its plan (Fig 3) and more especially in its

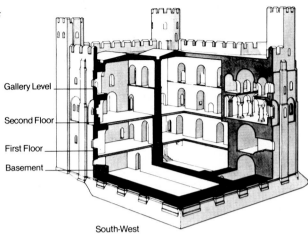

FIGURE 3 (OPPOSITE) *Floor plans of the White Tower, c 1100*

Gallery Level

Second Floor

First Floor

Basement

South-West

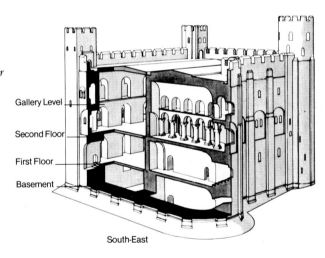

FIGURE 4 (RIGHT) *Cut-away illustrations of the White Tower from south-west and south-east*

Gallery Level

Second Floor

First Floor

Basement

South-East

apsidal projection at the south-east angle housing the chapel (which may represent a change from the original intention) there is nothing else like it in Europe save only at Colchester in Essex (Pl III), which is even bigger in its overall dimensions but otherwise resembles the White Tower so closely that it, too, must be the work of the Conqueror's reign and conceivably of the same master mason. The derivation of the two buildings is unknown, though they may be modelled upon the vanished tenth-century great tower in the castle of the Norman dukes at Rouen (demolished in 1204), and beyond that may derive from the late Carolingian palaces of the Frankish kings.

The Conqueror's White Tower is certainly

PLATE III *The great keep at Colchester from the south-east*

likely to have been finished at latest before 1100 when it is reported that Ranulf Flambard, bishop of Durham, was imprisoned in it by Henry I. Meanwhile it must have seemed as inappropriate to contemporaries as it may to us that so grandiloquent a building should be enclosed only by timber palisades to north and west in addition to its banks and ditches, and the argument is strengthened now that it is known that the Roman city wall stood on its other two sides, south along the river as well as east towards the open country. In such circumstances more importance than has been customary in histories of the Tower should probably be attached to the statement in the Anglo-Saxon Chronicle that William Rufus caused a wall to be built about the Tower on 1097—'This was in every respect a very severe year, and over-oppressive with bad weather, when cultivation was due to be done or crops to be got in, and with excessive taxes that never ceased. Also, many shires whose labour was due at London were hard-pressed because of the wall that they

built about the Tower, and because of the bridge that was nearly all carried away by a flood, and because of the work on the king's hall that was being built at Westminster, and many a man was oppressed thereby'. There seems no good reason to take the Old English word *weall* as meaning only (another) earthen rampart in this context: Rufus was not a man to do things by halves, and the passage is known to be authentic in relation to the king's works at Westminster, where his great hall when completed in 1099 was the largest then standing in England and probably in Europe. It may well be significant, also, that at about this time, and probably in 1097, the canons of St Paul's Cathedral thought it worth their while to obtain from Rufus a confirmation of their exemption from work on the castle of London (as upon the city wall and bridge) first granted them by the Conqueror.

By about the year 1100, therefore, it is likely that the first phase of the tower's architectural history was complete (Fig 2), the White Tower dominating all and already giving its name to the whole, with a bailey close about it (close especially to north, east and west) already walled in stone—and doubtless towered also, as the Roman wall to the east certainly had towers or bastions upon it, one of which survives in the footings of the present, and later, Wardrobe Tower (p 71 below). We may probably assume two gateways, one west towards the city, and one, a watergate, from the river. The only considerable space within the bailey, between the White Tower and the river front, we may suppose to have been occupied by the precursors of those palace buildings other than the keep itself, which certainly later stood there until the seventeenth century, in what was to become the inner ward of a greatly expanded castle.

It also seems likely that this first phase of the Tower's architectural development lasted for almost a century until the reign of Richard I (1189–99). Rufus's successor, Henry I (1100–35), certainly built and strengthened many castles both in England and Normandy, but there is no record of any substantial operations here, and much

FIGURE 5 *Elevation drawings of the White Tower from each of four sides*

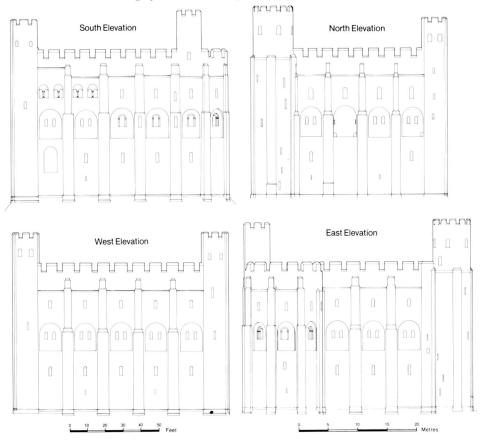

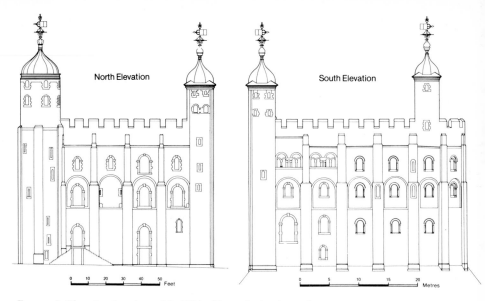

FIGURE 6 *Elevation drawings of the White Tower in the sixteenth century*

of his work elsewhere took the form of adding to existing castles stone-tower keeps such as London already possessed. He may, however, have added the forebuilding to his father's White Tower (p 60 below). In the political troubles of Stephen's reign (1135–54) the custody of the Tower and the control of the city was often a vital issue, but again there is no record of substantial works. Indeed, references to the Tower in some of the better-known documents of the reign evidently reflect, in the terminology of the time, the fortress of *c* 1100 already described, with its two-piece plan of a contemporary keep-and-bailey castle. Thus the first charter of the Empress Mathilda (Stephen's rival) to Geoffrey de Mandeville in 1141 grants him, amongst other things, the custody 'of the Tower of London with the little castle which was Ravenger's', but in her second charter, and in Stephens subsequent charter to the same earl in the

same year, this seemingly enigmatic phrase is replaced by the more normal wording of 'the Tower of London with the castle which is beneath it'. The distinction (emphasizing the dominant importance of the former) between the tower and the castle (*turris et castellum*) may seem odd to us but was quite common form at the time, and thus Henry I had granted, forty years before, 'the city of Colchester and the tower and the castle' to Eudo the Dapifer. The principal interest, therefore, of the Empress Mathilda's first charter in the history of the Tower of London lies in the name of Ravenger who, it is thought, may have been an early Norman constable of the Conqueror's day when the White Tower had not yet been added to the castle.

Henry II (1154–89), like his grandfather Henry I, was also a great builder of castles (witness Dover), but again it is almost certain that no major works were carried out here by him, although the Wardrobe Tower (Pl IV) has been attributed to his time on architectural grounds. William fitz Stephen, it is true, who wrote a contemporary life of the martyred archbishop Thomas Becket and provided a detailed description of late twelfth-century London in the course of it, assures us that his hero, as chancellor to Henry II, carried out important works at the Tower for his royal master with admirable dispatch (so great was the noise, he says, that a man could scarcely hear the man next to him speak). It seems, however, that we must take this with a pinch of salt, for the Pipe Rolls of the Exchequer, which survive annually throughout Henry's reign and record at least almost all his expenditure in England, know nothing of any such large undertaking though they faithfully and impressively record the king's works elsewhere. Their record is of maintenance and repair, and their occasional specific references to individual parts of the fabric seem again to echo the castle of the first phase—the White Tower and the chapel within it, the 'houses in the bailey', the kitchen, bakery and gaol.

Very substantial works indeed, however, were put in hand at the Tower of London early in Richard I's reign, evidently by his chancellor, William Longchamp, Bishop of Ely, who was placed in charge of the kingdom when the king went on crusade, and it is clear that these involved the first of three major extensions of the whole area of the castle to be carried out in the next century (Fig 2). The Pipe Roll of Richard's second year records in a special account the huge sum of £2881 1s 10d spent upon 'the work of the Tower of London' between 3 December 1189 and 11 November 1190 (a little over £1150 being the total recorded cost of King John's completely new castle

at Odiham in Hampshire some twenty years later), and the contemporary chronicler Roger of Howden states that in 1190 Longchamp 'caused the Tower of London to be surrounded with a moat of very great depth'. The same excavations by the Department of the Environment in 1964 which revealed the Conqueror's original ditch north of the White Tower (p 5 above) also showed that at about this time it was enlarged and deepened (to over 6m) and continued thus in a south-westerly direction towards the present and later Beauchamp Tower. Further, it is known from architectural evidence that the present Bell Tower (p 44) belongs to this period, as the Wardrobe Tower may also (p 71), while, in addition, excavations in 1958 revealed that the characteristic plinth of Longchamp's Bell Tower, consisting of seven Purbeck marble offsets, continues along the base of the existing south inner

PLATE IV *The ruined Wardrobe Tower*

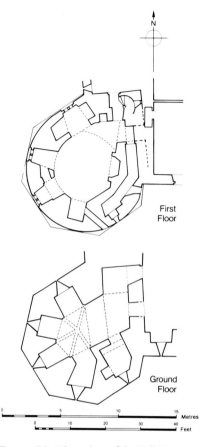

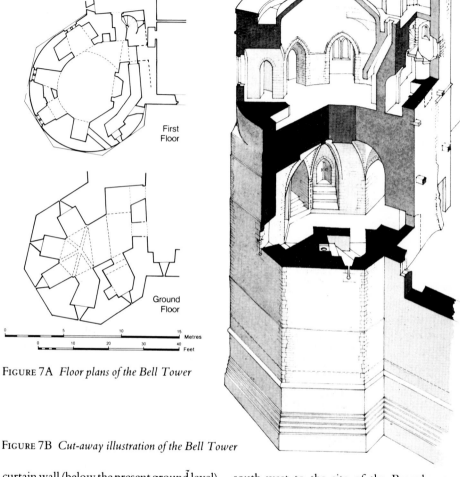

FIGURE 7A *Floor plans of the Bell Tower*

FIGURE 7B *Cut-away illustration of the Bell Tower*

curtain wall (below the present ground level) as far as the later Bloody Tower, thus dating that wall (which has other ancient features) to the same period. In short, the work of 1190, which may well have continued over several years, consisted primarily of a great new ditch on at least two sides, starting at the point of the Conqueror's ditch just north-east of the White Tower, and running south-west to the site of the Beauchamp Tower and south to the Bell Tower, with a stone curtain along the same line, this time certainly towered, and turning east at the Bell Tower to run along the river front, where it doubtless joined up with Rufus's earlier curtain of 1097 and the former Roman city wall in the area of the later Bloody and Wakefield towers. As a result, the area of the castle to the west was almost doubled, encroaching upon the city, and whatever remained of the western perimeter of the Conqueror and William Rufus now became an inner defence, further protecting what now becomes, and henceforward remains, an inner bailey and an inner sanctum of regality, housing the palace buildings subsidiary to the White Tower itself. To the east the limit of the castle still remained the line of the former Roman eastern city wall, though by this time the wall itself must have been much restored or rebuilt, and it is possible that Longchamp himself now both rebuilt it and enlarged the ditch in front of it. Indeed some memory of this work was preserved at Holy Trinity, Aldgate, where the compiler of a fifteenth-century cartulary referred to encroachment in this area by 'the outer wall and new ditch of the Tower', which, he wrote 'were built by the bishop of Ely as justiciar during Richard's absence in Jerusalem'—though in this he may have been confusing Longchamp's work with the much more extensive works and encroachments of Henry III and Edward I which followed in the thirteenth century. Meanwhile, both Roger of Howden and the later chronicler Matthew Paris (writing in the thirteenth century), observe with some satisfaction that the unpopular bishop failed to fill his new ditch with water from the Thames, and the archaeological evidence from the excavation of its northern length confirmed this point also.

Important as were the works of Richard I's chancellor, William Longchamp, in the evolution of the Tower, they were vastly exceeded by those of Henry III and his son, Edward I, in the course of the thirteenth century, and it is they who between them are chiefly responsible for the castle as we know it today (Figs 1 and 2). During Henry's long reign (1216–72) a total of £10 000 is recorded as spent on the Tower, and the general scope of his work is known even though its exact sequence and the degree of its completion is less clear. Major operations began about 1220 (when the king himself was still in his minority) when two towers were commenced. One of these was certainly the Wakefield Tower (Fig 8A, B, Pl XIX, XX), then called the Blundeville Tower, which was evidently built in two close phases between 1220 and c 1240, the chapel or oratory incorporated in its upper floor being painted and provided with a screen at its entrance in 1238. The other, specifically a smaller tower, was only less certainly the former Lanthorn Tower to the east (p 72 below), damaged by fire in 1774, pulled down in 1777, and now replaced by a nineteenth-century tower of the same name on a slightly different site. This was being roofed with lead in 1225–26. These two towers, it will be noted, stood at this date at the water's edge, and stood also at the two southern angles of what had been the original bailey of the castle and had now become the inner ward containing the palace buildings. A new curtain wall was also built between them, replacing perhaps that built by Rufus in 1097 and ultimately going back to Roman times. The lower courses of this thirteenth-century wall still remain east of the Wakefield Tower and are of one build with it. They contain, close to the tower, a postern (Pl V) which gave the king private access to his personal apartments in the palace, amongst which the upper floor of the new Wakefield Tower, with its oratory, formed his inner or privy chamber (Pl XX).

Other known works of these two decades of the 1220s and 1230s are likewise almost all connected with the inner bailey, and served to improve and bring up to date this

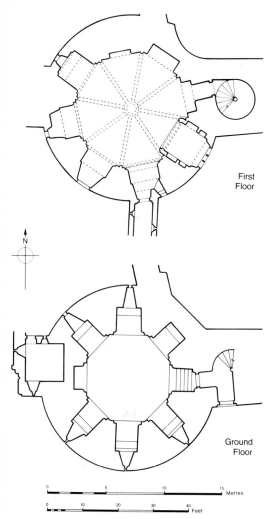

First
Floor

Ground
Floor

0   5   10   15
Metres

0   10   20   30   40
Feet

FIGURE 8A *Floor plans of the Wakefield Tower*

filled in (though now recently revealed again by excavation). The Coldharbour Tower, or gate, itself, of which only the foundations now remain, is presumably of this date also. In the growing complex of the castle, it stood as the inner landgate giving, and barring, access to the inner and palace ward. Immediately to the west of the Wakefield Tower and integral with it (though with no communication between them), another gateway was built which is now incorporated in the Bloody Tower (Pl vi) whose outer or southern archway towards the river is of this date. This, like the postern already described east of the Wakefield Tower, was at this time a watergate, for in Henry III's day the river washed the whole south front of the castle from the Bell Tower to the Lanthorn (and beyond, as we shall see). The new gateway was also guarded by the majestic strength of the Wakefield Tower close beside it and, inside, by the heavily fortified Main Guard wall already described.

Within the royal sanctum of the inner ward itself there was much rebuilding and refurbishing in the 1230s and also later. There is reference to a new kitchen in 1230, and the great hall (whose ruined structure is shown on the 1597 plan, lying along the south curtain east of the Wakefield Tower —Pl vii) had been virtually rebuilt by 1234 when it was whitewashed externally. In 1241 there was a new saucery, 'large and fair', built between the hall and the kitchen. The king's great chamber had been whitewashed externally together with the hall in 1234, and a few years later was fitted with new window-shutters decorated with the royal arms. We hear also of the queen's chamber whose walls were ordered to be whitewashed and painted with pointing and flowers in 1238, though two years later they were to be wainscoted and painted specif-

oldest part of the castle. Thus the Main Guard wall, with its formidable line of loops, running north from the Wakefield Tower to Coldharbour (Fig 1), is of one build, albeit in two phases, with Wakefield. It replaced whatever older defences stood here, the Conqueror's original ditch having been, it is now known, by this time already

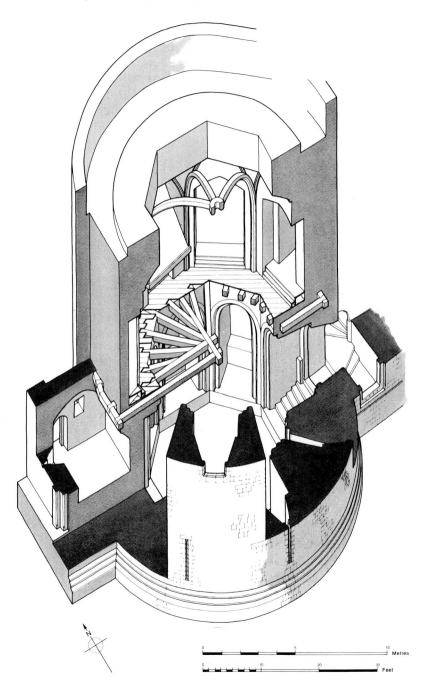

PLATE V *The Wakefield postern as discovered in 1957–58*

ically with roses. The Wakefield Tower itself, as explained above, formed part of this residential complex of increasing splendour, and so also, of course, did the Conqueror's great White Tower, whose entrance (at first-floor level) was on its south side from this inner ward. In 1240 orders were given to whitewash it (a custom from which it derives its name) and for its leaden drain pipes to be extended to the ground so that its white surface should not be stained by rainwater from the roof.

Meanwhile in or about the year 1238 another and even more important series of works was begun which, with various breaks and setbacks caused by natural causes (as we shall see) and by the political troubles and civil strife of 1258–65, continued to the end of the reign and, in a sense, beyond to overlap with the great works of Edward I. What was involved was the enlargement of the whole area of the castle to the east, north and north-west, and the consequent building of a new, towered curtain-wall about its new perimeter, from the Lanthorn to the Salt Tower and so round to the Bell Tower (Fig 2), with a new ditch beyond on the three landward sides. The southern curtain from the Bell Tower to the Lanthorn Tower inclusive, it will be understood, was already there by 1238, the earlier and western section built by Longchamp joining up with Henry III's wall of the 1220s and 1230s in the area of the present Bloody Tower (p 15 above). All this, moreover, however much restored and rebuilt, remains to this day the main, but now inner, curtain of the castle still further enlarged by Edward I (p 22 below), who rebuilt the western section between Devereux and Bell Towers and placed his great Beauchamp Tower in the midst of it. (The principal modern rebuildings are the Flint, Brick, Constable and Lanthorn Towers and the section of the curtain wall from the Lanthorn to the Salt Tower—Fig 1).

So large an extension of the Tower meant that to the east it broke out of the confines of the ancient and originally Roman city wall, whose line is now marked by the Bowyer, Wardrobe and Lanthorn Towers (Figs 1 and 2), and to the north and north-west took in an area of the city which included the parish church of St Peter-ad-Vincula, first mentioned in 1128–34 when it was already closely associated with the Tower but not then enclosed by it. Compensation had to be paid for such encroachments, and in 1239 a total of over £166 is duly recorded as paid to the neighbouring prior of Holy Trinity, Aldgate, the master of St Katherine's Hospital, and others, 'for the damage sustained by the wall and ditch of the Tower of London'. The actual beginning of the work is presumably marked by a payment in the previous year of £10 for a palisade made 'outside the Tower near the king's new works there'. A new quarry was opened in 1241, probably at Reigate in Surrey, and a Flemish expert, Master John le Fosser, was engaged, evidently to ensure

that the problem of filling the moat with water from the Thames, which had defeated Longchamp's engineers some fifty years previously, was this time successfully solved.

Not long after the beginning of this great operation a setback occurred which is both interesting in itself and informative about the plan and arrangement of Henry III's castle. The contemporary chronicler Matthew Paris relates, not without some satisfaction, that in the night of 23 April 1240 'the stonework of a noble gate which the king had built at great expense, fell to the ground . . . as if it had been struck by an earthquake', and that, exactly one year later at the same hour, the king's new wall about the Tower fell also. Of the second incident Matthew Paris has a fanciful version involving the agency of St Thomas Becket, and writes in terms of the whole new wall collapsing, but it is now supposed that it was a section of the western wall towards the city which fell, in the vicinity of the new gateway. The Elizabethan Stow (writing, of course, much later) in his *Survey of London* states that the collapsed gate was on the west side of the castle, and it is clear that it stood in fact on the site of the present Beauchamp Tower built by Edward I (Pl VIII and p 23 below). The main approach to the castle from the city along Great Tower Street is lined up to this day on this point where Henry evidently intended his principal outer gateway to stand. Such a gateway would have stood, however, at or close to the north-west angle of Longchamp's ditch of the 1190s, which in turn no doubt accounted for its collapse. Certainly when, some years ago, excavations were carried out north of the Bell Tower, the footings and foundations of the curtain there were found to be of quite exceptional size and solidity, as evidence, no doubt, of the precautions later taken by the masons of Edward I to prevent a repetition of the disaster which had befallen the wall and gate-tower of Henry III. According to Matthew Paris, Henry at once gave orders for his gateway to be rebuilt and more securely, though we have no other evidence of this being done and as late as 1253 there is what may be a relevant reference to 'the whole breach of the bailey' then blocked by a palisade. Nevertheless, large-scale works are known to have continued at the Tower off and on until the end of Henry's reign (with some break in the troubled years of political upheaval and civil war between 1258 and 1265), and it must seem very unlikely that a collapse in so crucial an area as the curtain towards the city, and at so prestigious a point as the main landward gate, was not made good in the thirty years and more before Edward I's rebuilding and remodelling of this section after 1275 (below).

In the course of the decade 1275 to 1285 Edward I undertook another great programme of works at the Tower, and one which again greatly extended the whole area of the castle, this time on all four sides including the river front to the south (Fig 2). That this was no mere continuation and completion of his father's original intentions is shown by the filling in of the latter's ditch, the construction of a new outer work in its place with another and greater moat beyond it on the landward sides, and the provision of new and more elaborate main entrances both from the city and the river. The cost of it all was prodigious, a recorded total of some £21 000, which is twice the recorded total for Henry III over the entire length of his long reign of fifty-six years, and which—though spent on a fortress-palace already large and strong before he began —exceeds the recorded cost of each of his brand-new and splendid castles in Wales (e.g. Conwy, Harlech, Beaumaris) save only that of Caernarfon (£27 000).

Amongst the new work to be begun at once was the digging of the present moat, the first of the extant building accounts, for the period May 1275 to December 1276, furnishing the huge sum of over £2484 spent on the wages of labourers (diggers and hodmen) for that alone. By the time it was finished, in or soon after 1281, the wage bill amounted to some £4150, and to this there must be added the wages of another Flemish expert—this time, a Master Walter of Flanders—the purchase of heavy timbers for piles and shoring, and the payment, once again, of compensation to those whose property was taken in for this third extension of the Tower's whole area. Much of the soil from the digging of the new moat must have been used for the infilling of the old one, but there is reference in the accounts to the sale of quantities of the 'king's earth', including clay to the London tilers, presumably for the making of bricks and tiles. The new outer wall on the inside edge of the moat and washed by the Thames on the south, forming the new outer ward, was low when built (it is now much heightened) and in the nature of a revetment wall at least on the three landward sides. The lofty inner curtain with its towers rose above and behind it to give covering fire. The outer curtain had no towers along its landward sides, although the lower half of Legge's Mount was part of this work. The lower half of Brass Mount seems to have been added subsequently. On the south, the Byward Tower and St Thomas's Tower, the Well Tower and the Develin Tower were originally all the work of Edward I in this period

(Develin was modified in 1679 and later, and the Cradle Tower was added by Edward III in the fourteenth century—see p 29 below). In this new river front of the castle, Edward I also provided two posterns or privy entrances, one east of St Thomas's to go with his father's postern east of Wakefield and immediately behind it, and the other immediately east of the Byward Tower. The former has vanished: the latter was rebuilt as a tower in 1350 and as such it still remains, though remodelled by Henry VIII in the sixteenth century (pp 31, 33 below).

Of the towers along the new river front, St Thomas's (which only much later came to be called the Traitors' Gate) was a water-gate supplanting the Bloody Gate behind it which now became an inner landgate and was altered accordingly (p 50 below), for the whole of Edward I's outer ward along the south (the present Water Lane) was made-ground from the river. St Thomas's Tower (Figs 1 and 2) was another of the first works to be begun, referred to on the first account of 1275–76, and evidently nearly finished by 1278 when coloured glass was fitted in its windows and carved and painted statues set up on the outer face of its 'great chamber towards the Thames'. It was connected by a bridge (the present bridge is a nineteenth-century reconstruction) with the upper storey of the Wakefield Tower, which had formerly been Henry III's inner chamber, and thus in its residential capacity served as a grand addition to what had been, and perhaps was still intended to be, the best and royal suite of palace accommodation. The Wakefield Tower itself, which somewhat lost both its military *raison d'être* and its dominant proportions by these alterations and the raised level of the new outer ward, may have been altered at its topmost level and even heightened in consequence, but

the theory that the whole of its upper storey was built or rebuilt at this time by Edward I is no longer tenable.

The new and elaborate western entrance by land from the city (Figs 10 and 11), with its right-angled approach via drawbridges and a barbican or outwork constructed in a spur of the great moat (later called the Lion Tower and very like the barbican at Goodrich in Herefordshire of similar date), and so via more drawbridges through the two twin-towered gateways of the Middle Tower and the Byward Tower, was also begun at once in 1275, and was probably finished by 1281. In that year the accounts refer specifically both to the completion of the western inner curtain towards the city and to the building of the Beauchamp Tower in the midst of it ('the large tower with the two turrets in the middle of the said wall'). The Beauchamp Tower stands on the site of Henry III's land-gate (p 21 above), which explains its immense width, and could not be built to block that entrance until the new western entrance was finished or in use. The tower is also an evident insertion in the wall which is not quite properly aligned on either side of it, and this, too, seems to be explained by the accounts of 1281 which refer to the completion, not the building, of a wall which already stood to the height of the embrasures and loops which run along its entire length—'in the work of the great stone wall towards the city formerly begun in its foundations and standing up to the first loops of the said wall'. The western curtain was thus of two phases, the first, including the shooting gallery, having been built some years before, the exceptionally

PLATE VII (OVERLEAF) *The Tower of London in 1597, as surveyed by Haiward and Gascoyne*

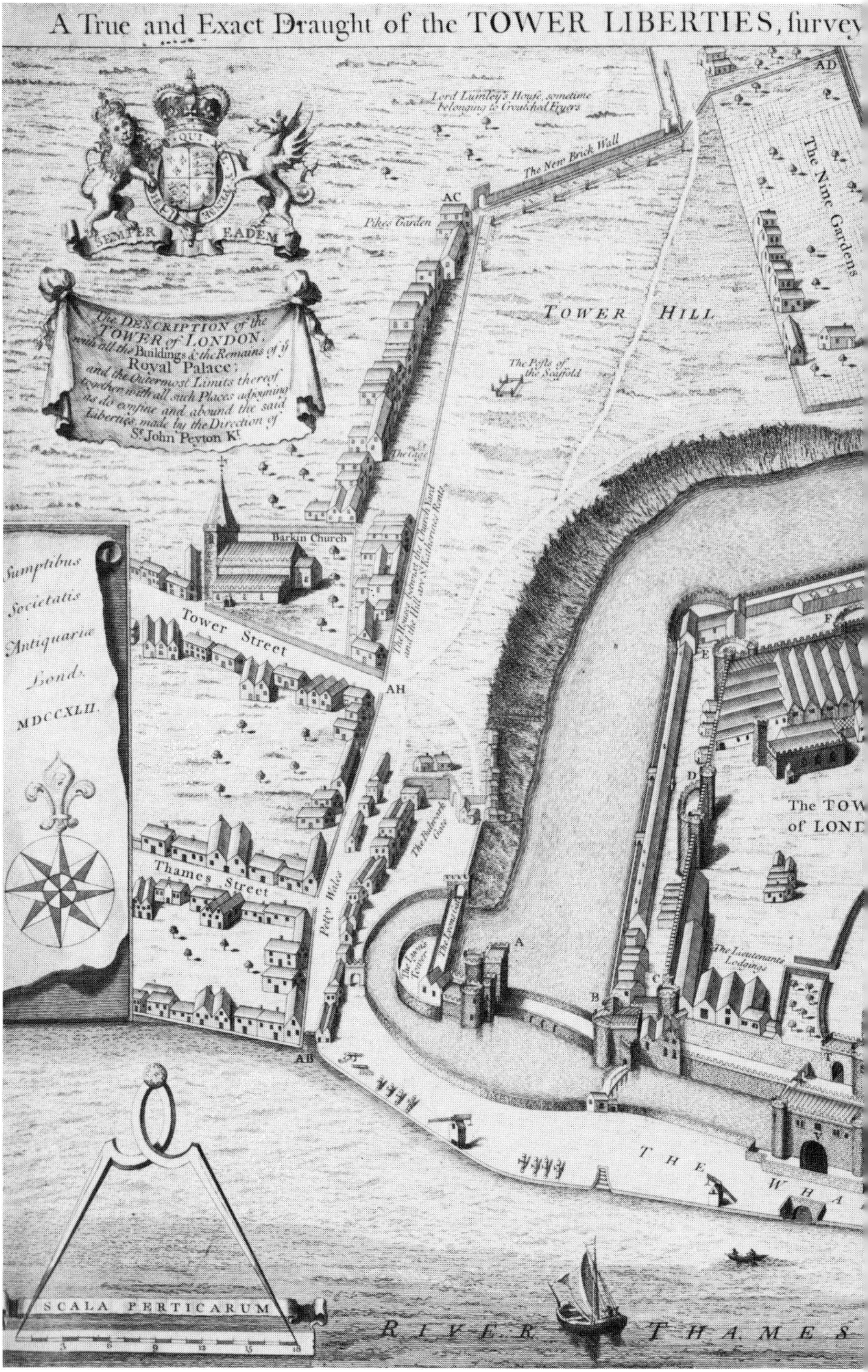

QUI

SEMPER EADEM

The DESCRIPTION of the TOWER of LONDON, with all the Buildings & the Remains of y Royal Palace; and the Outermost Limits thereof together with all such Places adjoining as do confine and abound the said Liberties made by the Direction of S.r John Peyton K.t

Lord Lumley's House, sometime belonging to Crutched Fryers

The New Brick Wall

AD

The Nine Gardens

AC

Pikes Garden

TOWER HILL

The Posts of the Scaffold

The Cage

Barkin Church

Tower Street

The House against the Church Yard and the Hill are Weathercocks Rents

A

AH

F

E

Sumptibus Societatis Antiquariæ Lond. MDCCXLII.

The Bulwark Gate

Peter Wales

D

Thames Street

The TOW
of LOND

The Iron Gate
The Rounds

A

The Lieutenants Lodgings

B   C

AB

THE WHA

SCALA PERTICARUM

RIVER THAMES

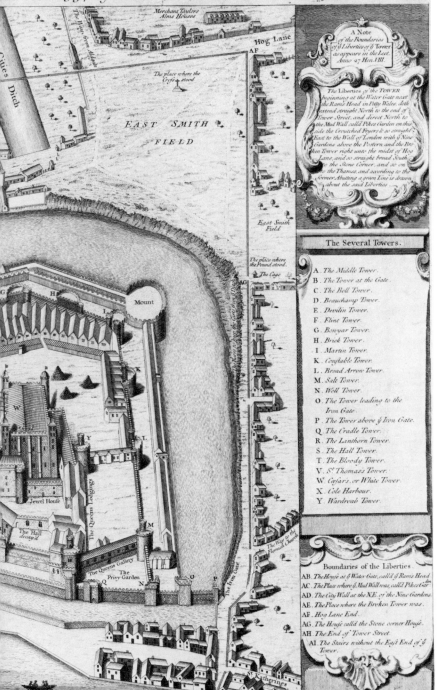

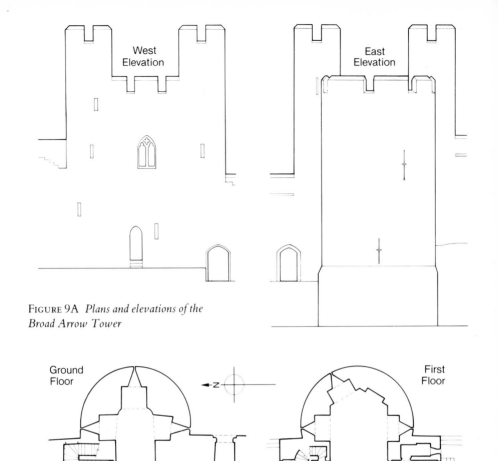

FIGURE 9A *Plans and elevations of the Broad Arrow Tower*

West Elevation

East Elevation

Ground Floor

First Floor

broad foundations no doubt integral with the infilling of Henry III's moat to avoid any possible repetition of the collapse of 1241 (p 21 above).

It has yet to be noticed that there were also further and subsidiary defences provided by Edward for his new outer ward in the form of cross-walls with gates, most of them still visible on the 1597 plan (Pl VII)—two, one north and one east, behind the Byward Tower, a pair on either side of

St Thomas's, and two again, one north and one east with vestiges remaining, at the south-east angle by the Salt Tower. The king also, like most of his predecessors and successors down to the sixteenth century, improved and extended the palace buildings of the inner ward in accordance with his own tastes and needs. Finally, and as an indication of the necessary self-sufficiency of a medieval castle (and indeed of any great residence of the age, secular or ecclesiastical),

Edward also had mills constructed across each mouth of his new moat, west towards the city and east towards St Katherine's. They were water-mills, and possibly tide-mills, worked by the sluices of the moat over which they stood.

Thus by 1285 and at Edward's hands the Tower of London had become, not only one of the finest castles in the land, which from the building of the Conqueror's White Tower it had always been, but also a great concentric fortress (one line of defences within another) of thirteenth-century fashion, well worthy to be compared with a Beaumaris or Caerphilly. It had also reached the point of its maximum development, and was, in spite of subsequent mutilation, the castle that we see today. The remainder of its architectural history, therefore, is largely a matter of the maintenance of the existing fabric combined with occasionaly relatively minor additions and alteration, until the demolitions, dilapidations and restorations of the modern period from the seventeenth century onwards.

Edward I himself entirely rebuilt the church of St Peter-ad-Vincula (which Henry III had merely refurbished) between June 1286 and April 1287 at a cost of over £327. It is also possible that in the 1290s Edward I was responsible for the extension of the south outer curtain from Develin across the eastern arm of his moat to the Iron Gate and the small tower marked 'F' on the 1597 plan (Pl VII), thus presumably demolishing his water-mill there (above), but the documents relating to the extensive works at the Tower in the king's later years are far from clear, and it is possible that this alteration did not take place until the reign of Edward II (1307–27) or even that of Richard II (1377–99).

Edward II certainly rebuilt 'broader and higher' the southern outer curtain from St Thomas's eastwards, and is known also to have repaired and crenellated the four towers of the eastern inner curtain, i.e. (from north to south) Martin, Constable, Broad Arrow and Salt (Fig 1). Otherwise, a survey of the dilapidations taken in 1335, and the very extensive reparations which followed it at

FIGURE 9B *Cut-away illustration of the Broad Arrow Tower, c 1270*

a cost of some £800, suggest that this inadequate prince had neglected the maintenance of the Tower of London along with many other affairs of state.

Edward III, however, whose achievements as a great builder and patron of the arts rival or excel those, better known, of Henry III (and were carried out, moreover, in a context of success and military glory rather than of failure and political opposition), was not a prince to neglect a major fortress and principal royal residence prestigiously placed in the foremost city of his realm. Over and above the necessary reparations of his early years referred to above, several quite important works were carried out at the Tower during his long reign. All of them, save the improvement and maintenance of the palace buildings themselves, were associated with the south river front which was undoubtedly then the usual royal approach to the castle.

In 1336 the heightening and strengthening of the southern outer curtain begun by Edward II was continued and completed, i.e. this time from St Thomas's westward to the Byward gate-tower, the work including the refashioning of Edward I's postern behind the latter. The entire length of the southern inner curtain was similarly heightened, crenellated and repaired from the Bell Tower to the Salt Tower in 1339, and a new gateway was constructed in the same wall, between the Lanthorn and the Salt towers, in 1339–41. References to this gateway as situated 'between the king's chamber and Balliol's tower', together with others more ambiguous, in the accounts of

PLATE IX *Charles Duke of Orleans in the White Tower, from a manuscript of c 1500 in the British Museum. Note St Thomas's Tower in foreground and the palace buildings, including the hall, behind and to the right*

these years, seem to imply that 'Balliol's tower' was the contemporary name for the Salt Tower, and that the king's inner or privy chamber was now in the Lanthorn—though we are told that he had hitherto been accustomed to lie (*solebat iacere*) in Coldharbour (Fig 1) wherein his chamber had now (1341) been taken over by his queen and their infant son, i.e. the future Black Prince. Moreover, Edward III's new gateway in the south inner curtain was more or less opposite a new watergate from the river in the outer curtain. This handsome building, now the Cradle Tower (Fig 17, Pl XI), was constructed between 1348 and 1355—the Black Death no doubt delaying its completion. The two new gates presumably formed a pair now more convenient

PLATE VIII (OPPOSITE) *The Beauchamp Tower from the west, now partly concealed by the heightened outer curtain wall* for the king than St Thomas's and the Bloody Tower with their adjacent posterns further west, and there also seems to have been direct access from the upper floor of the Cradle Tower (now vanished and rebuilt in the nineteenth century) to the royal apartments in and by the Lanthorn, presumably by a bridge such as Edward I had built from St Thomas's Tower to the Wakefield. Elsewhere in the complex of the palace buildings Edward III altered and restored the great hall, which received a new roof and the remodelling of the north wall 'towards the high tower' (i.e. the keep) with the renewal of the windows in it. A new house was built for the king's chaplain by the chapel (presumably of St Peter-ad-Vincula) and a new house and apartments were also built for the constable. The constable's house, constructed at considerable expense between 1361 and 1366, clearly reflected the dignity of the office, and there is reference to the purchase of window glass 'worked with fleur-de-lys and borders of the king's arms'. It stood, probably on the site of an earlier constable's lodging, where the Queen's House now stands, that house (the Lieutenant's Lodging of the 1597 plan—Pl

PLATE X *A model of the Tower of London, as it may have appeared in the early sixteenth century*

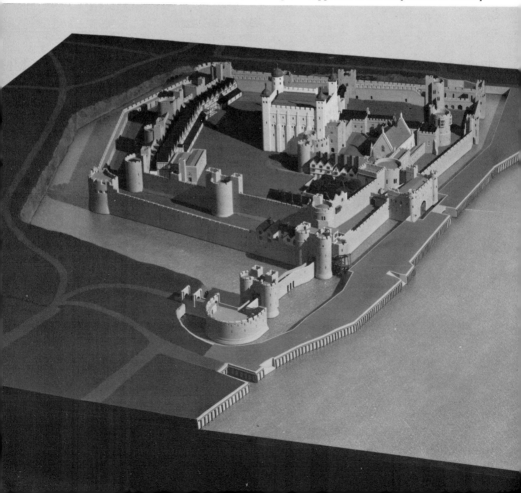

vii) being a sixteenth-century timber-framed rebuilding incorporating medieval masonry in its basement (Pl xxii and p 69 below). In Edward III's day it is likely that the constable's apartments also included the upper storey of the nearby Bloody Tower which were remodelled at this time (below).

The state entrance to the castle from the river through St Thomas's watergate and the Bloody gate behind it (p 23 above) was also improved by Edward III, for there is precise documentary evidence for the construction of the existing vault (Pl xii) in the entrance passage of the latter between 1360 and 1362 (by Robert Yevele, brother of the better-known master mason, Henry Yevele). This and other structural evidence also indicates that it was at this time that the upper stage of the Bloody Tower which by now had become a fully developed gate-tower of two storeys, was rebuilt and refurbished (pp 51–2 below). One further but minor entrance on the south front, the postern behind the Byward Tower, which Edward III had remodelled in 1336, he demolished in 1342 and rebuilt as a tower in 1350 (Pl xvi).

The Tower Wharf is another final feature of the fully developed castle which both survives to the present day and is largely the creation of Edward III (Pl x and Fig 1). Its history evidently begins in the time of his grandfather, Edward I, when a comparatively short length encased in timber piles extended from Petty Wales (the area immediately west of the barbican called the Lion Tower) to a point opposite the Byward Tower. This was extended in the same fashion as far as St Thomas's in c 1338–39, and was then reconstructed in stone between 1365 and 1370. It was not, however, until the last decade of the fourteenth century and the reign of Richard II that the stone-built

PLATE XI *The vaulted entrance (facing south) of Edward III's Cradle Tower*

wharf was extended the whole way along the river front to a point opposite the east end of the fortress.

Throughout the fifteenth century and the early Tudor period the Tower of London was kept in a state of repair and received certain minor additions and alterations, but there is no evidence of major works. It is known that Edward IV, in c 1480, added the brick Bulwark, i.e. the outwork on Tower Hill beyond the Lion Tower, further defending the principal landward entrance from the city (Fig 1). Richard III is credited with works at the Tower by Stow, but no evidence remains of them. Henry VII, the

first of the Tudors, was as frequent a resident at the ancient fortress-palace as most of his medieval predecessors had been since 1066. A splendid tournament was held here in 1501, and in 1506 the King's Gallery was built as an addition to the amenities of the palace which by now had two courts, east and west. The new Gallery ran from the Lanthorn Tower to the Salt Tower and figures prominently on the 1597 plan (Pl vii), where it is labelled (necessarily at that date) 'the Queen's Gallery' and appears either to have taken the place of, or to have incorporated, the inner curtain wall. South of it the 1597 plan shows the 'Privy Garden' (the earliest reference to a garden at the Tower—'in which my Lord takes the greatest pleasure'—occurs in Edward I's time when it had vines in it). In 1500–02 a stairway was made from the garden to the round tower 'where the king is accustomed to lie', which suggests that Henry VII's privy chamber was in the Lanthorn as Edward III's had evidently been (p 29 above). In this connection it is worth noting that both the 1597 plan and a fifteenth-century view of the Tower of London show prominently a chamber-block in this area between the Lanthorn and the great hall (Pl vii, ix). There is reference also in c 1501–02 to Henry VII's building or rebuilding of a tower (if new it must have been the last to be added to the castle) which seems to have been in the same area of the Lanthorn, and may possibly be the slender tower south of it, shown but not named on the 1597 plan and now vanished.

Henry VIII certainly remodelled the postern on the south front of the Tower behind

PLATE XII (OPPOSITE) *An 1821 engraving of the Bloody Tower gateway, showing the vault of 1360–62*

the Byward gate (p 31 above) by adding its wedge-shaped projection towards the river which, again, had gun-ports in it. He also, after a fire in 1512, and probably in c 1519–20, rebuilt the church of St Peter-ad-Vincula (on one occasion referred to, significantly for its former history, as 'the parish church within the Tower of London'), which accounts for the fact that it is now chiefly a Tudor church, albeit heavily restored in the nineteenth century. Between 1510 and 1520 he also rebuilt—in brick, and hence its modern name—the Brick Tower, on the north inner curtain (Fig 1) as a residence for the Master of the Ordnance, for whose ever-expanding department great new storehouses for 'all the king's majestie's store and provision of artillerie Ordinance and other Munitions' were built between 1545 and 1547 at a cost of more than £2894. These are presumably the great range of storehouses occupying the whole north side of the present Parade Ground on the 1597 plan (Pl vii). In 1540, after many requests and complaints, the Lieutenant's Lodgings, the former constable's house of Edward III (p 30 above), was rebuilt, to survive substantially as the present Queen's House (Fig 18, Pl xxiii).

Henry VIII was evidently both the last king to use the Tower as a principal royal residence and also the first to abandon it as such. In consequence particular interest attaches to the works put in hand here by his secretary, Cromwell, between 1532–33, because of the information they provide about the palace buildings towards the end of their long centuries of regal splendour. Most of the buildings mentioned are still shown on the 1597 plan (Pl vii), though because of the demolitions and alterations in the late seventeenth century of all save the White Tower itself we still cannot be sure of the exact arrangement of individual apartments. The documentation includes a detailed survey of the whole castle with two long reports to Cromwell on the progress of the works, while the works themselves comprised a general reparation of all the walls and towers as well as a thorough-going refurbishment and alteration of the royal accommodation within. The timber-framing at the back of St Thomas's Tower, i.e. the state watergate to the fortress-palace, was renewed, and, on the other (north) side of the palace court, the Coldharbour inner gate (Fig 1) was reported to be so decayed that it needed demolition in large part—presumably preparatory to its rebuilding though there is no record of this being done. Inside the palace court, there is no evidence either that the survey's recommendation to rebuild the 'olde hall' was carried out, and it is labelled 'Decay'd' and shown as ruined on the 1597 plan (Pl VII). The king's gallery (above p 33) between the Lanthorn and the Salt towers was repaired, together with the council chamber described both as 'within' and 'next unto' it (a small building with a double roof projecting to the north is shown on the 1597 plan). There was work also upon the king's Great Watching Chamber, his Great Chamber, Dining Chamber, the 'Chamber where his grace doth make hym ready', his Closet (i.e. Oratory, and provided with an altar and 'a desk for his grace to knelle upon'), and his Privy Chamber. The last-named was said to be 'next the water side' and to have previously been Henry VII's library. That king's bedchamber and council chamber are also mentioned as now converted to other uses, as is the former chamber of Lady Margaret Beaufort, mother of Henry VII and grandmother to Henry VIII. On the 1597 plan the king's lodgings (there, of course, called The Queen's Lodg-ings) are shown running up the east side of the inner ward from the Lanthorn to the White Tower and the Wardrobe Tower, and no doubt many of the apartments just named were within that range and, as we have seen, within the Lanthorn and its appendages. No buildings are specifically labelled as pertaining to the queen consort in 1597 though such had always existed. Among the apartments of the queen specifically mentioned in the documents of the works of 1532–33 are her great chamber and her dining chamber, and there is reference also to her garden, which was given a new timber bridge across the moat, towards St Katherine's, with a vane upon each of its six timber posts.

All these refurbishings and alterations were finished in time for Henry and Ann Boleyn to lodge at the Tower the night before her coronation in May 1533. After that, the king rarely if ever came again, and Anne, it seems, only for the nightmare of her imprisonment and execution. Indeed in the subsequent course of the sixteenth century the Tower of London became less and less a royal residence and, as Holinshed put it, 'rather an armorie and house of munition, and thereunto a place for the safekeeping of offenders, than a palace roiall for a king or queen to soiourne in'. Even the traditional practice of the king's lodging there the night before his coronation, thence to proceed in procession to Westminster the next morning, revived for Charles II in 1661, was thereafter discontinued, and indeed it was in his reign that the demolition of the royal palace in the Tower began, to make way for yet more Ordnance Office buildings, and to be rapidly completed under his successors.

It is not the purpose of this Handbook to recite the modern history of the Tower of London, but something must be said in outline, and with particular reference to the notorious rôle of the castle as a prison and place of execution, to bring its whole history into focus. In a sense, indeed, the real history of the Tower ends in the mid-sixteenth century. Any castle is first and foremost the fortified residence of its lord, and as such will also be, in an age of powerful and personal lordship, a centre of administration and local government. In the case of a great royal castle like the Tower, placed in the principal city of the realm in an age of powerful personal monarchy, it is not too much to say that the medieval government of the realm was concentrated in it whenever the king was in residence. In the course of

time some of the attributes of regality and some of the emerging departments of royal government settled permanently here—just as others more important, Exchequer, Chancery, Law Courts, settled at the neighbouring royal palace of Westminster—thus the Mint (from Edward I's time), a repository and manufactory of arms and armour, a treasury and repository of jewels and plate, a royal record office, even a royal menagerie. When Henry VIII abandoned the Tower as a royal palace in favour of his new Whitehall, and when, at the same time, the castle largely lost its military rôle, because of changes in the nature of warfare and, more important, profound changes in the whole nature of society, the Tower lost its medieval *raison*

PLATE XIII *The Tower of London in 1682*

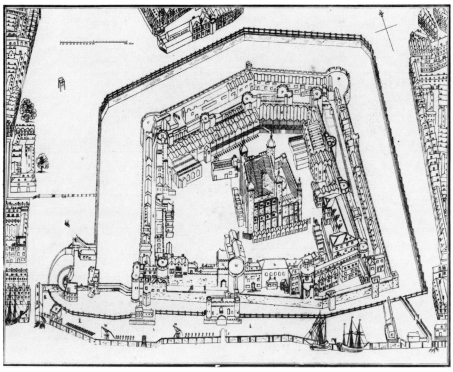

d'être and the various offices and departments already settled within it, the Ordnance above all, were left free to take over the whole, doing terrible damage to the medieval fabric in the process. The original purpose of the great building was forgotten, and an early guidebook to the Tower of London published about 1750, in listing the wonders to be seen there, says nothing about the castle which contained them. Only in the mid-nineteenth century did the Tower begin to be taken seriously as an 'ancient monument' of primary importance in its own right, and even then much of the restoration undertaken by Anthony Salvin and others was a damaging rebuilding.

The nineteenth-century romantic revival in the history of the Tower also has much to answer for in the manufacture of the morbid myth of a grim fortress-prison which reaches its apogee, perhaps, in Harrison Ainsworth's *The Tower of London* of 1840, though already in 1825 John Bayley had devoted more than half of his two scholarly volumes on *The History and Antiquities of the Tower of London* to a lingering account of the prisoners within it and the atrocities which befell them. Still an innocent visitor to the place today might be led to suppose, by guides and guidebooks, that it was built almost entirely by Tudor monarchs, exclusively for the incarceration, torture and execution of their innumerable prisoners. In truth this is a grossly misleading exaggeration of what in the main is a late and temporary phase in the history of the Tower. Most castles, as the seats of government and lordship, and as difficult to get out of as they were to get into, had a subsidiary rôle

as places of detention, and a great royal castle like the Tower of London was particularly convenient for the occasional confinement of high-ranking prisoners of state especially, for whom it could also provide suitably dignified accommodation. Thus the first recorded prisoner in its history is Ranulf Flambard, Bishop of Durham, in the early twelfth century, and amongst its most famous is or should be John, King of France, in the White Tower in regal surroundings, in the mid-fourteenth (see also Pl xi). It was only in the Tudor and Stuart periods, when the primary function of the Tower as royal residence and fortress declined and ceased, and the fabric of society was torn by events, that this subsidiary and occasional use became paramount, scarcely a tower or chamber without its prisoner. Nearly all those sad or defiant inscriptions, endlessly recorded and infallibly pointed out, date from the sixteenth and seventeenth centuries, and even then things were by no means always as the myth would have them. But when they were, and when the Tower is still presented to us as steeped in blood, we would do well to remember that political executions were not a medieval custom before the fourteenth century but reached some sort of apogee in the 'modern' period of the Tudors and the Stuarts, and that most of the blood shed inside the fortress (for the noblest in the land) or outside on Tower Hill (for those less elevated) belongs to that appalling age. Nor does the presence of those morbid ravens contribute to our understanding of the Tower of London which deserves a better memory than this.

Description

Though it would be better still to arrive royally by water and enter via the so-called Traitors' Gate (formerly St Thomas's Tower and the main state entrance from the river), the visitor does best now to approach the Tower of London by its equally ancient and main landward entrance from Tower Hill. Here, too, as one descends the slope the view of the castle is impressive to the left or east, though it is to be remembered that Edward I's wide moat should be filled with water (it was drained in 1843). Also, beyond the moat, the western outer curtain, which began in Edward's day as a low revetment wall, is built up much higher than it should be, and so masks the formidable inner curtain wall behind it to such an extent that even the great Beauchamp Tower in the centre is reduced in scale and power (Pl VIII).

From Tower Hill one enters via the elaborately defended approach constructed by Edward I between 1275 and 1281 to replace Henry III's main entrance on the site of the Beauchamp Tower (p 21 above), and consisting of a barbican or outwork, later the Lion Tower, and the two twin-towered gatehouses of the Middle and Byward towers. First and in front of all this the brick **Bulwark** (Figs 1 and 10), added by Edward IV in c 1480, has gone save for a few vestiges, and so has the **Lion Tower** itself save for its foundations. Here, or in what remained of it, the king's beasts were housed in the later stages of the Tower's history, to be one of the sights of London until they were removed in 1834 (to form the nucleus of the Regent's Park Zoo).

The **Middle Tower** (Figs 1, 10, 11) is a gatehouse basically of typical 'Edwardian' pattern, i.e. of two boldly projecting and cylindrical flanking towers on either side of the entrance passage. The towers have rectangular projections or turrets at the back which was originally timber-framed between them as the Byward Tower still is. The Middle Tower, indeed, though smaller in dimension, closely resembles the Byward Tower behind it, and neither was properly defended from the rear, unlike some of the great Edwardian gatehouses of this date and later. As it stands now, the Middle gate owes its external appearance as much to the eighteenth century as it does to the thirteenth, having been extensively refaced in Portland stone in 1717 when its upper storey levels were largely rebuilt. All its windows are of that date and the arms over the outer gateway are those of George I. In front of the gatehouse, to the west, there are substantial remains of the original causeway approaching it (visible from the moat), with a fine archway on the north side giving access to the lower mechanism of a turning bridge whose chases still survive at the base of the tower. The entrance passage itself has a timber ceiling and retains its original arches front and rear. There were two portcullises, one before and one behind the single gate placed forward. That gate was further defended by *meurtrières*, or murder-holes, in front of it and by low-placed arrow loops, one on either side from each of the flanking towers north and south, but there is no other gate at the rear. The

FIGURE 10 *Artist's impression of the Western Entrance at the end of the Middle Ages*

whole edifice was (and indeed still is) residential, with an entrance to each tower on either side of the passage a little beyond the middle. On the north side (the visitor's left) a doorway leads into a lobby with a vice or spiral staircase on one's right, ascending the tower to the upper levels of the whole gatehouse. In front there is a blocked pointed recess and, on the left, a passage down steps into the ground-floor room of the tower. This is a handsome, vaulted octagon, its vault, restored in the nineteenth century, having chamfered ribs of a single order and wall ribs. Six wall faces have sharply pointed embrasures for loops, but now only three loops (restored) remain, the other embrasures being either blocked or containing eighteenth-century windows. There was formerly a fireplace in the north-east face of the octagon where there is still a flue.

The ground floor room in the opposite south tower (currently used as a guard-room) is very similar. An octagon with a restored vault, it has a restored fireplace on the east side and the embrasures are again occupied now either by restored loops or by eighteenth-century windows. The latter have iron shutters with musket loops. The entrance lobby to this tower, off the south side of the gate passage, has a garderobe but no vice. The upper levels of the gatehouse, which could thus be reached only via the north tower, have been entirely rebuilt in the eighteenth century and now provide accommodation for a Yeoman Warder. There is only the one upper floor in the two main towers and across the gate passage, though there is a second floor in the two rear turrets.

The **Byward Tower** (Figs 1, 10, 11) is

the second and principal gatehouse of Edward I's main land entrance to the castle. It stands inside the moat on the line and angle of his outer curtain, loftier and larger in dimension than the Middle Tower in front of it. It too has lost its crenellated parapet in a modern rebuilding (eighteenth or early nineteenth-century) of its topmost level where there is much unfortunate brickwork, and it has been partly refaced, but otherwise retains more of its original appearance. The overall plan is again of two bold cylindrical towers on either side of the entrance passage, with rectangular projections or turrets to the rear, with timber framing still between them. The drawbridge in front of the gateway has vanished. The arrangement of the defences of the gate passage is the same as that of the Middle Tower, with, in sequence, a pair of low loops one on either side, an outer portcullis, *meurtrières,* the gate itself, and another portcullis behind it. There is no second gate or further defence to the rear. The two entrance arches, front and rear, are original, and the ceiling is timber. The doorways into the two towers, left and right, are in the same positions as those of the Middle Tower, and the accommodation inside, which was meant for residence, has a similar arrangement, though it is grander. The left-hand or north doorway opens into a handsome, square and vaulted lobby (not an oratory as has sometimes been stated), original but with its east window of two lights evidently a fourteenth-century insertion. On the left of the door is the entrance and skewed passage to the main ground-floor chamber on this side, and opposite is an original but blocked doorway and passage to the vice which, as in the Middle Tower, provides the only access to the upper floors. This vice, however, is now reached from outside

the tower at the rear or east, where the entrance to it is probably a sixteenth-century insertion. The main chamber itself in the northern tower is again an impressive octagon, in design much like the ground-floor rooms of the Middle Tower, but here with an original vault, an original fireplace with a restored head, and restored loops in most of its pointed embrasures, though the (off-set) loop to the south, covering the gate, is original. The embrasures facing west have small and later-inserted musket-loops near their heads. The corresponding chamber in the ground floor of the opposite south tower is again very similar, but with a modern vault and fireplace: it is reached from the gate passage via a vaulted lobby with a loop to the south and a garderobe opening off to the east. Again as in the Middle Tower, there is no vice on this side.

The first floor of the Byward is amongst the most interesting parts of the castle. On either side are the two octagonal chambers of the first-floor level of the twin cylindrical towers of the gatehouse, both with timber ceilings. That to the north is entered from the vice and has a restored but original fireplace to the north and three pointed embrasures to the west each now with a modern square-headed window, two with external iron grills. The tower-chamber to the south, is now partitioned off in brick from the central space of the gatehouse at this level, and is entered by a handsome door of sixteenth or seventeenth-century date. Its original features, too, are much more obscured by modern alterations, now decayed. The original fireplace, though mutilated, is in the south wall. Left of it (south-east) there is a large, modern, two-light window occupying the place of an original small window-opening, another of which is replaced by a modern square-headed

which may be original. It is richly decorated and painted in green with gold fleurs-de-lis. leopards and heraldic birds. The same pattern appears as the background to what was a finely painted Crucifixion of *c* 1400 on the south wall of the room. This, however, was mutilated in the sixteenth century when the present fireplace was inserted, its chimney-breast plastered and painted with a Tudor Rose in the place of the lost centrepiece of the Crucified Christ (Pl xv).

Finally at this level, at the south end of the portcullis chamber, and to the south of

Plate xiv *The Byward Tower portcullis*

the entrance to the southern tower-chamber, there is an original and acutely-pointed doorway eastward into a small, square and now panelled chamber which is the first floor of the southern rear turret of the Byward gate-tower. This is lit by altered or modern windows in the south wall, looking down on to the postern bridge below, and has two doorways in the east wall opposite the entrance. Of these, the doorway on the left or north, leads, via an original-looking arch (with a rebate for the door on the far side) and steps down, into the first floor of the Edwardian part of the adjacent postern tower (described below). The forced doorway on the right or south is clearly later and leads, via a very peculiarly shaped arch of very uneven springing, and steps up, into the lower of the two sixteenth-century timber-framed storeys added to the same Edwardian postern. On that side the archway is of more normal and acutely-pointed form, with a rebate for a door and a hacked-away hood moulding. It is possible that the first doorway originally led to the wall-walk of Edward I's southern curtain, and the second to the wall-walk of the same curtain as heightened by Edward III in 1336, though in that case the provision of the door rebates on the outside of the doorways is a little odd.

The existing upper floor(s) of the Byward Tower above first-floor level now contain private accommodation for a Yeoman Warder and reveal no original features, though there is a sixteenth-centrury door in the northern tower with moulded ribs and strap-hinges. Because of later alteration and rebuilding the original elevation of the gatehouse is, in fact, far from certain, though it is possible that the main structure, apart from the two rear turrets, had in the beginning two floors only.

PLATE XV *First-floor chamber in the Byward Tower. Note the Tudor flue, mutilating a medieval Crucifixion of c 1400*

On passing through the Byward gatehouse the visitor enters the outer ward of Edward I, commanded by the inner curtain with the Bell Tower (p 44 below) at its south-east angle. Mint Street, or the western outer ward, runs to the north on one's left, and Water Lane, or the southern outer ward is straight ahead, both originally blocked by cross-walls and gates now vanished (Figs 1, 11). Immediately on the right, abutting the Byward Tower and standing between it and the castle bookshop, is a small postern tower with a handsomely vaulted entrance (Pl XVI). Edward I had originally provided a postern gate, an informal private entrance,

here through his outer curtain. This was altered by Edward II, and then rebuilt as the present postern tower by Edward III (pp 31, 33 above). To this Henry VIII added the existing bold and wedge-shaped salient projecting southward towards Tower Wharf, while at some date, probably also in the sixteenth century, two timber-framed storeys, jettied with bowed-out windows, were added to the original tower of Edward III. One may now enter, via a four-centred arch, the entrance lobby of Edward III with its ribbed vault and a lion's mask in the central round boss. On the right (west) there is a porter's lodge. Beyond the porch are two

PLATE XVI *The Byward postern, inner entrance lobby (Edward III)*

passage-way, with gun-loops, one forward, one west and two east (Fig 11). In the west wall a large and heavily restored doorway opens on to a timber platform from which a drawbridge gave on to the Wharf. The opposite, east side of the passage is now screened off in modern brick to form storage space with modern ablutions, and here an inserted eighteenth-century wooden stair-case leads to the floor above which originally could only be gained from the Edward III postern tower. At this level there was at least one other gun-port forward, but all original features are now hidden by (eighteenth-century?) panelling and the screening off of the staircase to the south. The present panelled room communicates to the north with the upper floor of Edward III's postern, also panelled, and thence there are steps up via a pointed doorway (with a rebate for the door on this side) westward into the first floor of the southern rear turret of the Byward gate-tower (described above).

Opposite the castle bookshop and in the corner of Mint Street and Water Lane stands the **Bell Tower** (Figs 7 and 11), so called at least from the sixteenth century when the alarm bell for the garrison was rung from it (though the existing bell-cote near its summit is seventeenth-century, and the bell inside it dated 1651). This great tower, and the inner curtain wall running from it east-ward as far as the Bloody Tower, are basically Longchamp's work of the late twelfth century and the reign of Richard I. Both have the characteristic plinth of seven Purbeck offsets, which has been revealed by excavation at their junction. Many of the particular features of the tower are explained if one remembers not only its early date but also that, when built, it stood at the exposed and crucial south-west angle of the castle's outer defences (Fig 2), with

archways, one beyond the other, with segmental-pointed heads, the leaves of the wooden gate (now sixteenth-century?) opening between them and hinged on the outer or southern of the two. Beyond this again, at least in Edward III's time, there was formerly a drawbridge: the rebate for this is still visible in the outer face of the southern or outer archway, and it may have been worked via two holes still in place above it, one in the centre of the ceiling between the two archways and the other centrally above the head of the outer arch. Next, beyond the outer archway, a straight joint on the right or west reveals the addition of Henry VIII's salient. This at this level was internally a spacious, brick-lined

PLATE XVII *Ground-floor vaulted chamber of c 1190 in the Bell Tower*

are still visible in the top stage suggests that there was only a short interval between those phases. The interior of the ground or first floor (ie above the solid base) can now only be reached from the interior of the Queen's House, and it is at once to be noted that since at least the sixteenth century there has been no communication between this floor and the one above save via the interior of that house. The present entrance at this level from inside the house, however, was originally just outside it to the north, for there is no doubt that the house has been widened northward in the modern period. One enters through a wide arched doorway, which is original but cut about, and down five wooden steps into a sort of large lobby, irregular in shape like every part of the interior. On the right (north) the wall is brick, which may represent the blocking of access to the wall passage of the western inner curtain. The rear (east) wall left of the entrance has been rebuilt and refaced more than once, and has a blocked doorway, hacked about and now square-headed. An opening contemporary with the tower must have given access to the original staircase which has totally disappeared between the ground and first floors. Left of this again, or south, there is a round-headed entrance, now mostly in brick, to a spacious inner lobby for a garderobe. This has a pointed barrel-vault, an original splayed embrasure with a restored loop to the south, and the garderobe in a recess in the west wall. Marking what is in effect the division between the whole entrance lobby and the chamber itself, there is a broad, skewed, two-centred arch. The chamber beyond (Pl XVII) was originally grand like the lobby. It is an irregular pentagon in plan, vaulted with plain square ribs springing from moulded corbels with carved foliage (three

the city to the west and the river to the south washing its base; and also, again, that probably from the beginning it was incorporated with the constable's lodging on the site of the present Queen's House. It is certainly now incorporated with the Queen's House, forming part of its accommodation, and is thus not open to visitors.

The Bell Tower stands some 18m high on a solid masonry base which itself rises some 5m above the original river level, and with two storeys above the base. Up to the level of the first floor inclusive it is octagonal in shape, but thereafter cylindrical. This rather awkward change may suggest that it was built in two phases. The early form of the blocked two-light windows which of which remain) and with a foliated boss at their central and acutely pointed intersection. In the walls there are four corresponding embrasures, again acutely pointed, each slightly different and originally stepped up with high sills and plunging loops. That to the west is now blocked and that to the north fitted with a window and its sill hacked away. Here there is displayed the prayer book of Sir Thomas More, with his manuscript notes upon the open pages ('To have continually in mynd the passion that Chryste suffered for me . . .'). More, the former chancellor of Henry VIII, was incarcerated in this room for 15 long months before his execution on 6 July 1535.

Entrance to the upper floor of the Bell Tower is now either from the upper storey of the Queen's House or from the wall-walk of the western inner curtain (Elizabeth's Walk). One now enters, either way, into a modern porch which is contrived out of the south end of the wall-walk, and so passes into the tower itself through an original pointed doorway at first closed from the inside but later altered to close from the outside. Immediately on the left is the vice which now only begins at this level and ascends to the roof. One step down, a narrow passage leads into the entrance lobby, which should be open on the right into the first-floor chamber but in fact has been walled across and fitted with a modern door. On the left (east) and opposite this modern door there is a handsome, chamfered doorway, now bricked up but which can only have led into an early constable's house at first-floor level. Straight ahead and opening out of this entrance lobby there is a long and skewed stone-flagged passage running, via a loop (covering the outer face of the south inner curtain) and two doorways, through the thickness of the tower

wall to a garderobe, barrel-vaulted and with another restored and altered loop to the south. The main chamber within the tower at this level, roughly circular in plan, still shows signs of its intended distinction. Thus the rear arches to the four window embrasures (though each one is slightly different, as on the floor below) are double pointed or two-centred and have a moulded order which is continuous to form a string course between them. All, with the possible exception of the southernmost, which now at least is blocked and has a skewed window to the south-east, had rather elegant double or two-light windows though they now have eighteenth-century rectangular replacements. Between the two westernmost embrasures there is the interesting feature of a blocked wall passage which must have given access to a further window or loop on this exposed south-west angle of the late twelfth-century castle. The northern window embrasure has deep recesses on both sides, of uncertain purpose. In the adjacent north wall, near the entrance to the room, there is an inserted, fourteenth-century, square-headed cupboard with a chase for a shelf. There is also a fourteenth-century fireplace, now with an ugly brick head in place of its hood, in the east wall. The floor, of stone flags supported by the vault beneath, gives the appearance of having been lowered at some date. The present domed roof is a seventeenth-century heightening and beneath it the line of the original ring-beam for a timber ceiling can still be seen. There is only one inscription in this tower, on the wall by the vice and dated to the late sixteenth century.

To proceed straight on down Water Lane in what is an easterly direction, leaving the Byward Tower and its adjacent postern behind and the Bell Tower on one's left, is to reach the triple complex of St Thomas's Tower (*alias* the Traitors' Gate), the Wakefield Tower and the Bloody Tower (Figs 1 and 12), and also to approach the Conqueror's White Tower by the most informative route via the last named. As one does so it is essential to remember that the whole of Water Lane or the south outer ward is made ground from the river, added by Edward I who built the outer curtain on one's right, and that in consequence, before his time, all the south inner curtain and its towers on the left, of whatever date, were washed by the Thames from whose waters they rose (pp 19, 23 above and Fig 2).

Thus **St Thomas's Tower** (Figs 12, 13) was built on south outer curtain by Edward I, between 1275 and 1279, as a watergate to replace Henry III's watergate of the so-called Bloody Tower behind it, then left high and dry by the new outer ward. It was intended as the state entrance from the river in an age when kings and princes, as well as lesser men, used the Thames as a principal and convenient highway. Still called St Thomas's Tower on the 1597 plan (Pl VII), it only later became the 'Traitors' Gate' as part of that morbid myth which sees the Tower exclusively in terms of imprisonment, torture and execution. In plan resembling the former barbican and watergate on the east front of the Louvre in Paris (attributed to Philip Augustus, 1180–1223), it is a low oblong tower originally of two storeys only, boldly projecting into the river (the Wharf was not here until the fourteenth century—p 31 above), with two further-projecting turrets at the southern angles and the entrance in the middle of the south or river front. Entrance was by boat into a water-filled basin (now happily water-filled again) over which the tower stands and which originally extended further back into

the outer ward, which was here barred by the two cross-walls with gates respectively to east and west (Fig 13). Two wings project backwards from the tower to enclose the basin, from which broad steps lead up into the outer ward, and there is a third and staircase turret at the rear (north) of the eastern wing. The back of the tower itself, which the visitor sees from the outer ward, is timber-framed between the two wings, and broad stone arch spanning the basin. This timber-framing with its bowed-out windows is known to be a renewal of 1532–33 (above, p 34), but has been much restored since.

Now the residence of a Deputy Governor of the Tower and therefore not open to the public, St Thomas's had become until recently the residence of the Keeper of the Crown Jewels, the Jewels being then housed in the Wakefield Tower with which it communicates. The interior at first-floor level, is now much subdivided into modern rooms on two floors, but originally formed only two main apartments, hall and chamber, of a very high order (probably for the king—see p 23 above). The building accounts refer to 'the great chamber towards the water of the Thames' and 'the hall with the chamber above the gate over the water of the Thames'. They also refer to tiled floors, opening windows (*fenestres currentes*) fitted with coloured glass, and to painted statues set up on the river front. At this level also there were two small vaulted chambers in the two southern turrets, the eastern one being usually identified as an oratory. It is likely, therefore, that the eastern apartment at this level, with the oratory, was the great chamber, and the western, where there are traces of a former garderobe, was the hall. Below this level the three walls of the tower and its wings,

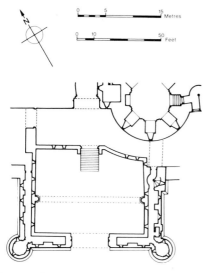

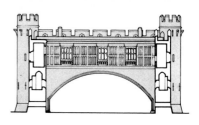

North Elevation

Ground Floor Plan

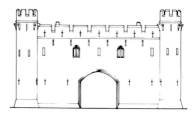

South Elevation

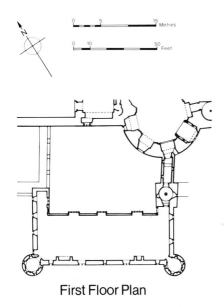

First Floor Plan

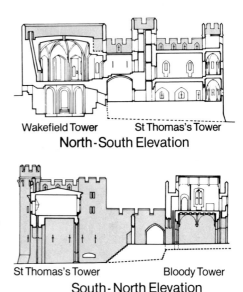

Wakefield Tower   St Thomas's Tower

North-South Elevation

St Thomas's Tower   Bloody Tower

South-North Elevation

FIGURE 12 (ABOVE OPPOSITE AND THIS PAGE) *Plans, sections and elevations of St Thomas's Tower with the Wakefield and Bloody Tower*

east, south and west, are pierced by mural galleries, which communicate with vaulted chambers in each of the southern turrets but stop, of course, on either side of the entrance portal from the river. Both east and west galleries are entered through doorways direct from the outer ward and the east gallery is also entered from the vice. They are liberally supplied with loops to cover both the river approaches to the gateway and the basin within it, and the eastern gallery has a garderobe. The river gateway itself could be closed by an iron sluice or portcullis and by folding gates. The former must have been worked from the chamber

FIGURE 13 (BELOW OPPOSITE) *Artist's impression of St Thomas's Tower and the river approach at the end of the Middle Ages*

above, however grand (cf the Byward and Bloody Tower portcullises), and the latter may have been worked from the galleries. The galleries have lost most of their original vaulting, hacked away when a mezzanine floor was inserted at that level into the whole tower to make a hospital of it in the late seventeenth or early eighteenth centuries (later still there was machinery in the drained basin for the drilling of cannon). Lastly, opening off the vice in the north-east turret there are two restored doorways, one above the other, giving access respectively to the bridge and its rampart-walk which cross the outer bailey to the Wakefield Tower. The present bridge is a late nineteenth-century replacement of an original feature, and in this way both the defences of the two towers were linked and also the domestic and palatial accommodation within them.

The **Bloody Tower** (Fig 14 A and B) is a composite building of three medieval phases, and its name, though of some antiquity, is very misleading. Although already

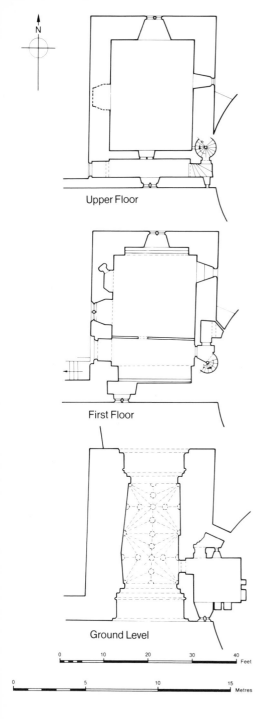

N

Upper Floor

First Floor

Ground Level

0   10   20   30   40
                          Feet

0   5   10   15
                          Metres

called the Bloody Tower in 1597, it was the Garden Tower in 1532 and there is no contemporary evidence to connect it with 'the Princes in the Tower' (the sons of Edward IV) who, if they were lodged here, and if they were murdered here, did not in any case meet a bloody end. This building, then, began as the watergate of Henry III in the early 1220s, constructed in the new south curtain then being built from this point (where it joins up with and continues Longchamp's work) to the Salt Tower, with its footings washed by the Thames. The new gateway must have stood in or across the early Norman ditch which had once formed the western limit of the castle (p 5 above and Fig 2), and was formidably guarded by the great Wakefield Tower (below) whose first phase is of one build with it. In the beginning, however, it is now clear that the Bloody Tower was not a tower proper but a mere gateway built almost entirely within the thickness of the new curtain, and in consequence only the present outer portal and the porter's lodge due east of it are of this date. There must have been, however, some superstructure for the working of the portcullis, and it is possible that this was the crenellated chamber in front of the Wakefield Tower referred to as under construction in 1224. The porter's lodge in this first phase was entered from the north via a causeway which skirted the ditch in front of the north-west quadrant of the Wakefield. Only some half a century later and in the time of Edward I did the gateway thus described become a gate-tower, when it ceased also to be a watergate as the result of the construction of the outer ward and of the new watergate of St Thomas's. The

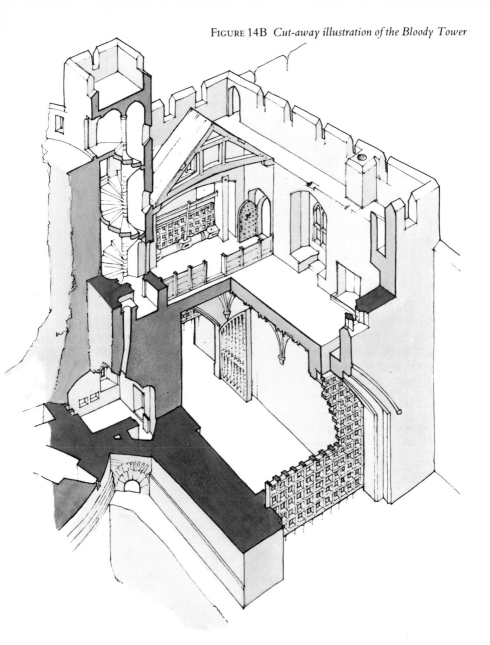

gate passage was then extended to its present length (straight joints in the side walls betray the sequence and the new structure stands upon the causeway of Henry III already mentioned) and the inner or northern portal is of this date. There must also have been a full superstructure added though this has disappeared, the present upper stage being a complete or nearly complete rebuilding by Edward III, who is known from documentary evidence to have inserted the present vault over the gate passage in 1360–62. Finally the tower was heightened in 1603 with the insertion of the third floor for Ralegh's imprisonment.

The Bloody Tower as it now stands is some 14m high and of three storeys with the top and parapet a modern restoration. It has lost something of its original proportions (Fig 14B)not only by the heightening of the early seventeenth century but also by the construction of the outer ward itself and the subsequent rising of the road level (some 1.5m of plinth originally showed below the sill of the outer gate). The gate passage rises slightly from south to north as the ground rises up from the river, and is slightly bent to the east (as a further indication of having been built in two phases). The inserted vault (Pl XII) was very fine, with lions' heads on the corbels and lions' masks in the bosses, though now clumsily repaired with Roman cement. It is very similar indeed to the contemporary vault in the Norman Gate at Windsor Castle. The passage was originally defended by two gates and two portcullises, one of each at either end. On the right or east, just inside the outer portal and obscured by the leaf of the outer gate when open, a modern doorway, probably replacing a fourteenth-century predecessor, leads into the porter's lodge. This is a small room, some 3m square, with an original flattened barrel vault. It had no communication with the Wakefield Tower until modern times when the present access was cut through. In the north wall there are the remains of a small original and rectangular window and of the original entrance doorway, blocked when the gate passage was extended to the rear

by Edward I. The fourteenth-century two-light window in the south wall was probably a loop in the beginning, and so was the doorway in the west wall now forming an entrance from the gate passage. The cupboards, of which there were formerly four, in the south and east walls are insertions, probably dating, like the fireplace across the north-east angle, from the sixteenth century.

The first floor of the Bloody Tower, as was probably always the case, can only be reached from outside, from the higher ground to the west and from the direction of the constable's lodging. Entrance is through what appears to be a fourteenth-century doorway into the portcullis chamber which may itself be basically the remains of Henry III's work at this level. This is now screened off from the main apartment by a timber partition of sixteenth or seventeenth-century date, presumably replacing an earlier one. The portcullis and its machinery (probably sixteenth-century) is still here beneath a broad and deep arch which supports the wall-walk above, and it is satisfactory to record that in 1846 the Duke of Wellington, as constable, refused to make this accommodation over to the Record Office (then housed in the adjacent Wakefield Tower) on the grounds that it contained one of the few working portcullises in England. There is a nineteenth-century window (which may replace something earlier) looking on to St Thomas's Tower. At the far (east) end of the portcullis chamber a doorway with a shouldered arch leads into a small lobby, with a garderobe opening off on the left (north) via a square-headed doorway, and a vice opening off half-right via a pointed archway. The vaulted garderobe is fourteenth-century and the vice, which has chalk blocks in it and only begins at this level, is an insertion, either of the fourteenth or the fifteenth century, to reach the roof.

The main chamber at first floor level (Pl XVIII) beyond the screen now principally shows fourteenth-century features of Edward III's work. It has the substantial remains of a splended floor of patterned tiles (packed about the edges with brick) dating from the 1360s and only recently revealed and identified beneath the grime of centuries. In the west wall there is a large window of the same date though the stone mullion and transom are insertions of 1603 and the head is cut off by the new floor then inserted. North or right of this window is a restored fireplace, again of the mid-fourteenth century, square-headed and with an original bread-oven in the right-hand side. The north wall of the room shows the arch of the northern portcullis (now gone) though this is now of nineteenth-century date, and the window on this side is now also entirely modern though it had at least a sixteenth-century predecessor (shown in Bayley's *History and Antiquities of the Tower of London*, i, opp p 262). The window in the east wall, looking on to the Wakefield Tower, is so restored as to remove any trace of a predecessor. The timber ceiling of the room is the recently restored floor of the room above, inserted, with some heightening of the tower, in 1603 for Ralegh's imprisonment. This room is reached via the vice already described. It has itself been heightened in the modern period and its present ceiling is nineteenth-century. The blocked window in its east wall is so restored as to be of uncertain date, but the north window is original, i.e. 1603 at this level. The south-west corner has been partitioned off to form an inner chamber, probably in the eighteenth century though this may

perpetuate an arrangement originally made for Ralegh. The rear or southern wall common to both the main room and the partitioned chamber is of stone, and the space behind it was the wall-walk of the southern curtain, taken in, so to speak, when the tower was heightened in the early seventeenth century. This is therefore now an enclosed passage (lit by a nineteenth-century two-light window looking down on to St Thomas's Tower on the south) with the inserted vice blocking it and ascending to the roof on the east, and the exit leading out on to the surviving open wall-walk to the west.

The Bloody Tower contains many inscriptions and its accommodation on both first and second floors has recently been furnished with some fine pieces appropriate to Ralegh's period.

The **Wakefield Tower** (Fig 8A and B) stands immediately east of the Bloody Tower and is integral with its first phase. Built in the reign of Henry III in two phases between *c* 1220 and *c* 1240, it is also integral with his new southern curtain from here to the Lanthorn and Salt Towers, and with his Main Guard Wall running north from the Wakefield to his Coldharbour Gate. Its position thus described, and confirmed by a glance at the Development Plans of the whole castle (Fig 2), emphasizes its original importance when built, as a great flanking tower at the south-west angle of the inner and palace ward, commanding what was then the river front of the fortress, and more particularly guarding both the main water-gate of the Bloody Tower and the king's privy postern in the south curtain immediately east of it, discovered by excavation in 1957–58 (p 17 above and Pl v). The Wakefield Tower, in fact, is by far the largest tower in the castle save only for the White Tower

of the Conqueror himself, and, further, it is known that the splendid accommodation inside it formed part of the royal suite in the contemporary palace buildings and included Henry III's inner or privy chamber at first-floor level. In a sense, the Wakefield was almost the donjon of Henry III's Tower of London, at once strong-point, principal residence and dominating feature, and, in so far as it contained at least part of the king's accommodation, replacing in function the White Tower, whose military eminence was in any case reduced by the growing complex of defences about it. Built in the latest cylindrical fashion, it closely resembles those *donjons circulaires* then so popular in France, and particularly favoured by Philip Augustus (1180–1223) at, for example, Falaise, Gisors, Châteaudun and the Tour de Coudray at Chinon. But by the fourteenth century the king of England no longer chose to lie in the Wakefield Tower; by the sixteenth century if not before it had become a repository of records and part of the Record Office (hence one of its several names, the Record Tower); and from 1870 the Crown Jewels were displayed in it. The immense damage and disfigurement caused by the latter use especially could only recently be made good after the removal of the Jewels to their present home in 1967, and now, since 1973, the tower has been re-opened to the public to reveal something of its former royal splendour for the first time in many centuries. Nevertheless, the great tower still loses much externally. The construction and building-up of the outer ward on ground thus gained from the river

by Edward I accounts for its present truncated look from Water Lane (only on the north do the recent excavations by the Main Guard show its proper stature on that side), the raising of the Bloody Tower beside it and the building of St Thomas's Tower in front of it by the same king still further reduced the dominance of its original proportions, and the bridge built at the same time to connect it with St Thomas's emasculated it. It suffered also much nineteenth-century restoration in its upper levels, where the bridge is now a reconstruction of that date and the windows an unfortunate contemporary exercise in 'medieval' pastiche. The evident change, however, from the ashlar facing of the lower storey of the tower to the rubble of the upper need not indicate that the latter was added or rebuilt at a later period but, rather, that ashlar was imperative at those levels of the structure which, on the south, were washed by the water of the Thames.

The original entrances to both floors of the Wakefield Tower are on the east side, and originally access was only from the palace buildings and the royal apartments therein, which communicated directly with the upper floor, or via Henry III's postern in the south curtain hard against the tower, which led direct into the lower floor or by a spacious vice 3m in diameter to the upper floor. Within, the recent work of reparation has revealed the original splendour of the lower apartment for the first time in almost 700 years (Pl XIX). The removal of the 1867 brick vault and other supports inserted to bear the weight of the iron cage containing the Crown Jewels in the room above, and the excavation of the original floor level by the removal of a reinforced concrete floor with two successive brick floors and other infilling beneath them, have almost doubled

the height of the room to its original lofty
6m and more, and similarly restored the
true proportions of its recesses and loops.
The excellence of the original masonry is
also revealed in these lower levels which
were so soon covered up. For while the
lower of the two brick floors probably dated
from the late sixteenth century, much of
the infilling beneath it was of late
thirteenth-century date, and thus represents
an early alteration (and debasement) of the
tower at this level, probably by Edward I
and to obviate flooding (which still sometimes occurs) caused when his new outer
bailey to the south impeded the drainage of
water into the river from the rising ground
to the north. The room itself is octagonal
in shape with a tall recess in each face. The
recesses are round-headed in spite of their
early thirteenth-century date (cf the Devereux Tower), and so misled many early
historians of the Tower to give this ground
storey a much greater antiquity. The eastern
recess contained the original entrance,
blocked by a false loop in 1880 and now
re-opened, leading by a broad flight of steps
down into the interior. The three southern
recesses have stepped-up and deeply splayed
loops, covering what was the water front,
of the very tall and narrow type (here
1.8m×38mm) then fashionable. In their
present state their upper levels, which alone
until recently were visible, have been
reformed but their lower levels are original.
The north and north-west recesses have

PLATE XIX *The ground floor of the
Wakefield Tower during restoration. The
line of the infilling can be clearly seen and
the consequentially preserved lower levels
of the loops. The steps on the left (east)
lead in from Henry III's postern*

rectangular windows high up. The western and north-eastern recesses were blank, as the latter still is, because they respectively backed on to the Bloody Tower gateway and the great hall complex of the palace buildings, but in 1880 a doorway (which has been retained) was cut through the former (when the original entrance opposite was blocked) into the porter's lodge of the Bloody Tower. The most remarkable single feature of the room is its timber ceiling, now an accurate reconstruction of the original which was carefully drawn by G T Clark before its destruction for the vault in 1867–69. Its complex ingenuity is better illustrated than described (Fig 8B), but it must be noted that its joists go far into the walls of the tower and were originally anchored in a ring-beam close to the outer circumference. This, having rotted over the centuries, could not be replaced, and in consequence a central post—which had an ancient predecessor to support the weight of the records which came to be deposited in the room above (p 35 above)—has been inserted although the original thirteenth-century ceiling is unlikely to have needed one.

The upper room of the Wakefield Tower has also had much of its former dignity restored to it in recent years after the removal of the Crown Jewels (Pl xx). Here, indeed, dignity is regality, for it is clear that this noble apartment was constructed as the inner or privy chamber of Henry III, and it is thus also the only part of the medieval palace accommodation to survive in something like its original state (discounting, that is to say, the much altered accommodation within St Thomas's Tower and the White Tower itself). The shape of the chamber is again octagonal, but it is ingeniously twisted in relation to the room below so that at this

PLATE XX *The first floor of the Wakefield Tower, Henry III's privy chamber, showing the fireplace, the blank north-east recess (which may have been for a chair of estate), the entrance (east) and the oratory*

level there could be four recesses (here with pointed arches) to the south instead of three. No medieval windows survive, however, the present windows being nineteenth-century and known to have replaced in turn Georgian sashes. The chamber is entered through the east recess and a tall, narrow, arched passage. In the adjacent south-east recess is an oratory (once separated by a timber screen provided in 1238) with aumbry, piscina and opposed sedilia (the northern cut through to make a doorway, probably in the eighteenth century). The next, southern, recess has evidently been altered from a window opening to receive the doorway leading to Edward I's bridge to

St Thomas's, and next to this an awkwardly placed and canted window has evidently been inserted at the same time. The next recess has only its modern window of two lights, and the next again, to the south-west, has a half-window (also modern) of one light to avoid the junction with the Bloody Tower. The north-west recess was originally a window but was converted into the present doorway to give access to the Jewel House in *c* 1870. Next and north, opposite the Edwardian doorway to the bridge, is the fireplace, an original feature with its plaster hood recently restored. The north-east recess, between the fireplace and the original entrance and opposite what were the three southern windows, is and always was blank, and it has been suggested that the king's chair of estate may have been placed here. The existing vault of this noble apartment is nineteenth-century, but it springs from original octagonal wall shafts (restored and with no capitals). Since no other traces of a thirteenth-century stone vault were noted by Clark before the works of 1867, it is quite possible that the original vault was wooden.

From within the Wakefield Tower the visitor may now proceed direct to the Wall-Walk along the south and eastern inner curtain via the Lanthorn, Salt and Broad Arrow towers to the Martin Tower at the north-east corner of the castle (Fig 1 and p 72 below). It is, however, more logical historically to deal next with the innermost ward of which the Wakefield forms a part. If, therefore, the visitor leaves the Wakefield Tower via the site of the vanished great hall, or having completed the Wall Walk retraces his steps to pass through the gate-passage of the Bloody Tower, he can see the north outer face of the Wakefield itself in its full original elevation from the bottom of the quadrant ditch dug in front of it on this quarter and recently re-opened. This ditch belongs to the first phase of the construction of the tower (1220–25?) and was soon after filled in. It was stopped to the east by the first phase of the Main Guard wall, of one build with the tower and carefully bonded in. Next, also on the right, comes the full extent of the **Main Guard Wall,** now ruined and so called after successive modern buildings which housed the Guard, the last of which was only removed after 1940. The whole wall is the work of Henry III in the 1220s and 1230s and formed then an inner curtain and the immediate defence on the west of the inner palace ward: its most notable feature is the formidable gallery of loops covering the approach up from the Bloody Tower watergate (as it then was). In front of it there is now revealed (by excavation in 1974–75) an early ditch which, though filled in by the time that the Main Guard Wall was built, has been left open as (almost certainly) the only visible remains of the original castle dating from the winter of 1066–67 (p 5 above). This wall ends near the **Coldharbour Gate,** of contemporary date and standing between it and the White Tower. The anomalous arrangement of walls in this area may possibly suggest the existence of an early landgate here of the time of the Conqueror or Rufus. Of Coldharbour itself only the foundations now remain, to show it as a gate-tower of typical thirteenth-century pattern with two cylindrical flanking towers, one on either side of the entrance passage. This then, was an inner gate giving and guarding access to the palace ward, to be passed through whether one entered the castle by Henry III's watergate at the Bloody Tower or by his intended main landgate on the site of the Beauchamp Tower (cf p 21 above).

The Conqueror's **White Tower** (Pl I and Figs 3–6) still dominates the castle as it was meant to do, though the size and complexity of the latter have vastly increased since it was first built. Its date and construction have already been discussed above (pp 9–12), as have also its purpose and nature as the original donjon and great tower of the castle, at once the military strong-point and containing the best residential accommodation, including that for the king himself on the top or second floor above the basement. In plan it is rectangular except for the apsidal projection at the south-east angle, housing the east end of the chapel, and except for the cylindrical north-east angle turret which houses the main vice or spiral staircase from basement to roof. Recent excavations have shown that it is possible that the south-eastern apsidal projection here represents a change of plan from an originally intended straight rectangle. The great tower measures 36m east and west by 32.5m north and south (which is very large indeed, though exceeded by Colchester), and is 27.5m high to the present battlements without counting the turrets. The walls are from 3.5 to 4.5m thick at the base with a splayed or battered plinth on three sides, south, east and west, accommodating itself to the rising ground level. There are four angle turrets, including one at the south-east where that angle of the great tower would be were it not for the apsidal projection, each now capped by a lead-covered cupola surmounted by a weather vane. Each face of the keep has the flat pilaster buttresses characteristic of its period, stepped back by two off-sets as they rise and dying into the main structure a little below the parapet. The material of the keep was rag-stone rubble (mostly Kentish rag), though septaria was chiefly used in the plinth: the ashlar dressings were originally Caen stone but are now Portland, for the exterior has been much restored, not least in the early eighteenth century which is responsible for the present form of most of the windows and doorways. The south front, however, facing the visitor who ascends the rising ground towards the keep from the Bloody Tower gateway, retains at its top level and at the west end high above the entrance, two pairs of little-altered original two-light windows, round-headed and each beneath a larger round-headed arch forming Romanesque arcading. On this front also is the original but now externally much altered entrance (described below), and the treatment of the windows at second-floor level (however much they themselves have been altered) seems especially apparent, each set in a large round-headed recess, one between each buttress, again to form a bold Romanesque arcading and a deliberate architectural emphasis upon the royal residential suite within.

The original entrance to the White Tower was at the west end of this south front, in the bay between the south-west turret and the adjacent buttress, and at first-floor level for security reasons. It has recently been re-opened, though externally in its early eighteenth-century form, that the public may now gain access to the keep as their royal rulers formerly did. It is gained by a modern timber flight of steps, and must in the beginning have been gained in similar fashion. At some stage, however, this was replaced by a stone forebuilding, i.e. a covered and defended stairway within a tower adjunct, of the kind normal with later twelfth-century tower keeps. Such a structure is shown in this position on the 1597 plan (Pl VII), as it is also on the well-known fifteenth-century miniature now in the British Museum (Pl IX) where it appears to have an early two-light window. Otherwise it has left almost no evidence, though later documents suggest its demolition in 1674 together with the remains of the Jewel House. The absence of any documentary references to its construction suggests in turn an early date for that, probably before the mid twelfth century.

In the course of time there came to be other adjuncts also to the White Tower. Probably the earliest was a long building

PLATE XXI (OPPOSITE) *The White Tower from the north-east*

PLATE XXII *An 1821 engraving of the White Tower from the north-east, showing the great annexe attributed to Edward III*

against the east face, and apparently engulfing the south-east apsidal projection, which again has left no trace whatever and has not yet been archaelogically investigated. It is shown on the 1597 plan (Pl VII) as a continuation of the line of buildings there labelled the 'Queen's Lodgings' (ie normally the king's lodgings), and it is shown very prominently indeed as a major building in the 1821 engraving of the White Tower

printed in John Bayley's *History and Antiquities of the Tower of London* (Pl XXII). Bayley described it as 'a low stone building which forms a wing to the main structure' and attributes it to Edward III—though no documentary reference to it or its construction has yet been found. Bayley further stated that 'it consisted formerly of one storey only, but has, within the last twenty years, been raised, and is now used as a repository for old books and papers belonging to the office of Ordnance'. G T Clark, writing in 1884, mentions this building and also attributes it to Edward III, though by his time it had been demolished (ii, 219). The 1597 plan also shows the 'Jewel House' hard against the south side of the White Tower east of the forebuilding, and this may be the Jewel House to whose construction there is documentary reference in the 1530s. It probably had, however, a late medieval predecessor in the house built for John Lowick or Ludwyk, keeper of the Privy Wardrobe in the Tower, in the reign of Richard II, and the slender tower slightly left and in advance of it on the 1597 plan also dates from that time and was 'the new tower called Ludwyktoure' in 1400. More demeaning were certain modern adjuncts to the White Tower, and thus Bayley in 1825 mentions a 'contemptible brick erection' against the west side of the keep and used as a guardroom. All these accretions, including the forebuilding, are now gone, and today the White Tower stands proud and free much as the Conqueror built it, although many external details, including windows, doors and facings, owe more to early eighteenth-century than eleventh-century masons.

Internally, save only in the chapel of St John on the second floor, the original residential purpose of the great tower, the *arx palatina* of William fitz Stephen's phrase (p 10 above), and the spacious Romanesque grandeur of its accommodation, are now obscured by the Tower Armouries which it houses. Alterations over the centuries have also taken their toll, and here it must be particularly emphasized that its original arrangement was of two floors above the basement (each being residential), and not three as now (Fig 4). As long ago as 1912

William St John Hope suggested that the present second and third floors were really the division of one floor rising through two stages (*Archaeological Journal,* lxix, 219), but the suggestion seems never to have been followed up until recently, though it is doubly important as affecting also the interpretation of the ruined keep at Colchester which in every way closely resembles the White Tower. This second floor, which contained the chapel of St John, was thus by far the grander of the two, and was undoubtedly the royal suite of accommodation within the tower.

Each floor, including the inserted third floor, is subdivided into three principal apartments: first by a cross-wall or spine-wall (a common feature in large rectangular keeps), running north to south, placed not quite centrally, and dividing the keep into two unequal parts east and west; and second, by an east–west wall cutting off the southern section of the eastern part only, to form the chapel (on the second floor) with its triforium above and its crypt and sub-crypt below, each with its apsidal projection (Figs 3 and 4). All floors from top to bottom, again including the inserted third floor, are served by the main vice in the north-east cylindrical turret and which ascends from the basement to the roof. There are also, as original features, two vices, respectively in the north-west and south-west angle turrets, which commence only at second-floor level to ascend to the roof. In addition a fourth vice, contrived in the thickness of the south wall, is evidently a fourteenth-century insertion chiefly to provide separate access to the chapel from outside the tower. It commences at first-floor level, where it was entered also from the vanished forebuilding, and ascends only to the second floor whence a mural passage leads off into the chapel's south aisle.

Although the visitor now enters the White Tower at first-floor level through the original southern entrance described above, it is logical to begin the description of the interior with the **basement** (Figs 3 and 4). This in fact is only partially below ground level on the north side, and not at all on the south because the ground level itself is sloping down to the river. It is divided into the three compartments common to each level of the keep, and its original use was undoubtedly for storage and other services (*not* prisoners), the well (12m deep) being situated in the western compartment. In more modern times it was still in use as a gunpowder store well into the nineteenth century, and the two main rooms east and west received their brick piers and brick vaults in the eighteenth-century (*c* 1730). The original access was only from the north-east vice and thus into the eastern and smaller of the two main compartments, which in turn communicates with the western compartment via a doorway in the north end of the west wall (which is the cross-wall of the keep) and with the sub-crypt of the chapel via an original doorway in the south wall. Four other entrances have been forced through into the basement direct from outside at various dates, in all cases except the last-noted through a former loop or lighting shaft. One is into the north-east vice, one each respectively into the eastern and western compartments through the north wall of the keep, and a fourth into the latter high up at the southern end of its west wall. This western compartment has also in its east wall a forced entrance through into the sub-crypt. All three compartments are now lit by modern recessed shoots in the outside walls bringing in light from the window embrasures of the floors above, three in the east wall, four in the west and one at the east end of the sub-crypt. Some traces of the original tall and deeply splayed recesses for loops, however, still remain. The west room had one in the south wall, now blocked but clearly apparent, two in the west wall, and one to the north in the place of the present forced exit. The east room also had one in the north wall where the modern exit now is, and at least one more in the north end of its east wall. The present steeply splayed recess at the east end of the sub-crypt comes closer to the medieval arrangement, though this too now has a shoot at the end of it (Figs 3 and 4). The sub-crypt itself is plain and largely featureless, though the entrance into it from the east room is original (and shows the jamb for a door) and the barrel vault over it still reveals the marks of centering. Of the two main compartments of the basement, the west room is now known as the 'Cannon Room' and contains various guns, while the smaller east room is the 'Mortar Room' containing mortars and other pieces of ordnance.

The **first floor** (Figs 3 and 4) was the lower and less grand of the two residential suites which the White Tower originally contained. It was thus supplied with garderobes and fireplaces, and we may suppose that its three divisions were, respectively, great hall on the west, great chamber on the east, and the crypt of the chapel of St John above serving as the chapel on this level. It is entered from outside via the original entrance to the keep, already described, into the western apartment or hall, now called the 'Sporting Gallery' (and formerly the 'Small Arms Room'). In addition to the exhibits which obscure its former function, this grand room has also two rows of eighteenth-century timber posts now supporting the ceiling. In the south wall, to the right or east of the main entrance, there is a round-headed recess which was originally a window embrasure but was altered in the fourteenth century to accommodate a vice then inserted. This ascends to the floor above and has its own doorway to the vanished forebuilding and the palace ward below. In the west wall, ie on the left as one enters, there are five round-headed recesses now fitted with (over-large) early eighteenth-century windows, with an original eleventh-century and round-headed fireplace between the third and fourth recesses. The north wall originally contained within its thickness two garderobes, one at either end, each entered through a tall, narrow round-headed doorway. Immediately above the right-hand opening, high up, there are traces of a blocked and later window. Immediately adjacent to the left-hand garderobe doorway, a lower and wider opening has been cut through in modern times to bring in light from the garderobe loop, itself converted into a window. Between the two garderobes, and rather more than half-way across the wall, there is a further opening, broad and arched, now closed by a screen and evidently a window embrasure of uncertain date. The east wall of the great hall is in fact the cross-wall of the keep. There was and is no opening through it into the crypt or lower chapel, but there were originally two doorways, one north and the other towards the south, leading into the great chamber, i.e. the principal eastern apartment. Between them were three deep and lofty round-headed recesses to form a kind of arcade and which only in modern times have been cut through to join the two rooms (Fig 3).

The eastern apartment or great chamber (substantially smaller than the hall because of the crypt or lower chapel across its southern end—Fig 3) is now called the 'Tournament Gallery' and was formerly the 'Record Room'. It, too, is disguised by the Armouries exhibits within it, and by two rows of eighteenth-century timber posts supporting the ceiling. Five arched openings pierce the west wall, as explained above, though in this room there were originally no recesses between the two doorways north and south. In the north wall there was a recess for a loop now converted into the main exit from the keep with a double flight of modern steps down into the Parade Ground. Right of this, in the north-east corner of the room, is the original but restored doorway leading, via a short passage, to the main north-east vice serving all levels. In the east wall there are three recesses for loops but now fitted with large early eighteenth-century windows like those in the hall, and between the second and third recess there is again a round-headed original fireplace. The south wall of the chamber is largely taken up by a very wide and round-arched recess which contains a restored doorway on the west leading into a lower chapel which is the crypt of the chapel of St John on the floor above. This is similar to the sub-crypt below it at basement level, but has a modern barrel-vault, a restored east window in the apse, and three restored window embrasures with modern windows in the south wall. Of these the two outermost embrasures are skewed, presumably to avoid weakening the wall too much at this level. The west end wall has a restored round-arched recess occupying almost its entire width. Finally, in the north wall just short of the apse (Fig 3) there is a small, nearly square, mural chamber, entered by a restored round-headed doorway with evidently sixteenth-century inscriptions on the jambs. In that period therefore, but of course not originally, this room was made to serve as a prison.

The **second floor,** (Figs 3 and 4), was originally both the topmost floor of the Conqueror's keep and the accommodation for the king's own majesty. A grand residential suite of hall, chamber and chapel, following basically the same plan as that of the first floor below it, there are or were several features marking its superiority and regality. First and foremost, as noted above, it originally rose through two stages to a double and lofty height, with a mural gallery encircling the outer walls at the level of the present third floor, which is an insertion, to join up with the triforium of the chapel which still rises properly through its two stages (Fig 4). Assuming, as we may, that Colchester followed the same arrangement, then both these great keeps of the eleventh century anticipated in this respect a treatment of their principal residential floors not uncommon in keeps of the twelfth, notably at Rochester, Castle Hedingham and Dover. Moreover, and now more obviously, it is this floor in the White Tower which, as at Colchester, is served by the splendid chapel (here of St John), to be described below. There are other though lesser features of superiority also. Thus the original window openings (replaced in the early eighteenth century by the present windows) could at this level be larger, each of two lights, in addition to the extra windows in the mural gallery above them (Fig 4). The garderobe provision on this floor is also better, with the pair in the north wall placed closer together by the doorway connecting hall and chamber, one of them directly serving the latter which also had another garderobe opening off the northern window recess in its east wall. Lastly, there commence on this floor two further original vices, respectively in the north-west and south-west angles, ascending via the mural gallery to the roof. Of course much of this royal splendour is now gone, masked above all by the inserted floor, but also by the rows of eighteenth-century timber posts placed in the two main rooms to support it, and also, it must be confessed, by the exhibits of the Armouries, however excellent in themselves. By these means the true purpose of the great hall and the great chamber are obscured to the casual visitor, and only in the chapel of St John, mercifully restored to its proper use since the nineteenth century, can one gain some concept of the White Tower as the first Norman king built it for himself.

The main western apartment or great hall, now called the 'Sixteenth-century Gallery' and formerly either the 'Weapon Room' or the 'Banqueting Hall', can be entered either from the inserted fourteenth-century vice in its south wall (which also leads to the chapel of St John) or from the eastern apartment. This vice, as on the floor below where it commences, has been contrived in a former window embrasure. There is another southern window embrasure next to it, and from this a mural passage heads off to one of the two original vices, respectively in the south-west and north-west angles, which commence at this level and ascend to the mural gallery and roof. The other is similarly gained by a mural passage from the northernmost window embrasure in the west wall. In all, there remain in this great room eight of its original nine window embrasures, five in the west wall, two in the north and one in the south, all round-headed and all fitted with early eighteenth-century windows. The absence of any surviving trace of a fireplace in the west wall, corresponding to the one on the floor below, in this the principal state apartment of the best and royal suite, must at least suggest a central hearth, and may therefore be additional evidence that this level was originally the top floor of the keep, rising to the roof. The east wall of the hall is the cross-wall of the keep, and has restored original round-headed doorways into the great chamber in the extreme north and two-thirds of the way to the south. At this level the surface of the wall was flat on this side, the three recesses between the doorways being on the other or chamber side, thus reversing the arrangement of the floor below for structural reasons (Figs 3 and 4). Here as there, all three recesses have been cut through in the modern period.

The eastern apartment or great chamber is now called the 'Medieval Gallery' and was formerly the 'Sword Room'. It was entered either from the main north-east vice or from the two doorways from the hall, just described, with the three round-headed recesses now pierced between them. The north wall contains, between the northern doorway and round-headed entry to the vice, a small round-headed doorway to a garderobe on the left, and, placed centrally and greatly enlarged in the fourteenth century, a window embrasure. There are three round-headed window embrasures, all with eighteenth-century windows, in the east wall: opening off the northernmost is a garderobe, and the space between the second and third to the south is occupied by an original round-headed fireplace corresponding to the one on the floor below. The south wall is plain, without the arched recess of the floor below (the wall being thinner at this level), and has in its west end the original doorway into the chapel.

The **Chapel of St John** (Pl II) is the most beautiful place in the whole Tower of London, and though, housed in a keep, inevitably small by the monumental standards of Norman ecclesiastical architecture, has all the austere serenity of Romanesque. Characteristically desecrated in the mid-sixteenth century, and thereafter used as a repository of records until the mid-nineteenth century, when (according to Clark) it nearly became a tailor's warehouse, it was then restored to its present condition which comes close to its original appearance. In length 17m and 9.5m wide, it is aisled with apse and ambulatory, the latter continuing the aisles about the east end, and rises through two storeys with a plain triforium or tribune as its upper stage. The vaulted aisles and ambulatory are divided into thirteen bays by the columns of the main body and by responds forming an arcade on the outer walls, each bay having a groined vault. The main body of the nave is barrel-vaulted as is the triforium passage (with eight small windows north-east, east and south to bring in extra light), and there is a semi-dome over the apse. The fourteen columns of the main arcade are cylindrical and stand closer together about the apse, to produce there arches more stilted than the semi-circular arches of the nave and thus give a certain architectural emphasis to the east end which is repeated at triforium level. The capitals of the columns form a most important series and a microcosm of the influences at work on the Anglo-Norman architecture at the time of the Conquest. Eight are of the simple block-shaped type with fluted chamfers, two have primitive volutes, one is pseudo-Corinthian, one is a cushion capital and two are double cushions. In addition, the two western capitals have a geometric enrichment upon their abaci, and eleven of the fourteen have the rare embellishment of Tau crosses, or T-shaped projections, which are applied to all types of capital in the chapel except the cushions. These last must represent an English influence derived from Germany and strengthen the suggestion that the Norman masons of the Tower were moved here from Edward the Confessor's Westminster Abbey. The west wall of the nave and aisles terminated in shallow round-headed recesses, though that in the south aisle was cut through in the fourteenth century to give separate entry from outside the keep via the vice then inserted in its south wall as described above. The original entrance from the king's great chamber is in the westernmost bay of the north aisle. The chapel is well—or, perhaps one should say in this age, sufficiently—lit by handsome and original window openings (the windows being modern with glass from Strawberry Hill) in the apse (three) and the south aisle, as well as by the additional light coming from the triforium.

The present **third floor** (Fig 3) is an evident insertion of uncertain date, a tempting documentary reference to the construction in 1603–05 of a new floor in the White Tower for a 'powder house' not necessarily relating to this particular alteration. It may therefore follow that some at least of the memorable historial events said in the older guidebooks to have taken place in its main western apartment, the so-called 'Council Chamber', must be found another place. It is certainly to be noted that a principal feature of this floor is a barrel-vaulted mural gallery, which joins up with the chapel triforium to surround the whole, and marks in reality the second stage of the principal residential floor below. It is significant also that there are no garderobes or fireplaces at this level, that the main north-eastern vice is not entered direct from the eastern apartment but only from the mural gallery—

which similarly provides the only access to the chapel triforium—and that at this level the cross-wall of the keep between the two main rooms forms itself into a true arcade of five equal round-headed openings as opposed to the two doorways and three larger pierced recesses of the two original floors beneath.

Both rooms, east and west, were occupied by the Record Office until the mid-nineteenth century and have since been taken over by the Armouries. The larger, western room, the former 'Council Chamber' and latterly 'Horse Armoury', is now called the 'Tudor Gallery'. The two vices respectively in the north-west and south-west turrets give access to it via the mural gallery, which also traverses the round-headed window embrasures, two to the north, five to the west and two to the south. The windows themselves, in the outer wall, are of early eighteenth-century date except on the south where some of the original two-light fenestration is preserved. The east room, formerly the 'Tudor Room' but now called the 'Seventeenth-century Gallery', has a modernized window opening in the north wall and three round-headed embrasures in the east wall with early eighteenth-century windows. All are traversed by the mural gallery. The roof, to which the three vices at this level ascend, is closed to visitors. The top of the cylindrical north-east turret housing the main vice was used as an observatory for a brief period in 1675 before John Flamstead, Charles II's 'astronomical observator', moved on to Greenwich.

In the great space of the main ward about the White Tower, where even the palace courts, the very heart of the medieval castle, and the Coldharbour gate which gave access to them, have gone (Fig 1), there is little now which is medieval in date, or which

PLATE XXIII *The Queen's House, formerly the Lieutenant's Lodgings, from the north-east*

would be recognized by Edward I or Henry VII, save for the towered inner curtain itself which will be further described below.

The **Queen's House** stands in the south-west corner adjacent to the Bell Tower (Figs 1, 18 and Pl XXIII). Its name is misleading since it has in fact never been a royal residence but is now the house of the Resident Governor, and was formerly the Lieutenant's Lodgings as shown on the 1597 plan with the Lieutenant's garden to the east of it (Pl VII). The present house was built in 1540 (p 33 above) and is an L-shaped timber-framed structure, resting on the south and west curtains behind it, with four gabled bays in each range, the westernmost bay of the south wing being mostly obscured by the west wing. Altered in the seventeenth century and restored in the modern period, the house shows much of its timber-framing externally (with ogee curved braces and carved bargeboards) except where masked by brick facing at ground-floor level, the addition of single storey buildings to form the present porch and office, and a late seventeenth-century facing, with windows, beneath the jetty of three of the four western bays. There was also a brick and timber early seventeenth-century staircase turret against the easternmost bay of the south range, shown on older photographs and views but removed in 1960. Internally, the most notable feature of the house was a rather grand first-floor hall, open to the timber roof, running north and south in the penultimate western bay of the south range. This, however, was floored in the very early seventeenth century, its inserted upper floor now being the Council Chamber, with an elaborate memorial tablet by the fireplace erected in 1608 to commemorate the frustration of the Gunpowder Plot. The upper floor of the house is now reached by a handsome late seventeenth-century or early eighteenth-century staircase. Beneath the south range of the present Tudor dwelling there are substantial remains, still visible towards the east, of a fourteenth-century house, running east and west, which is thought to be the constable's lodgings of Edward III's reign built in 1361–66 (p 30 above). It is as least likely, moreover, that this earlier house in turn had a predecessor and that the residence of the medieval constable of the Tower was always on this site from Longchamp's day (p 45 above), running east and west and integrated with the Bell Tower as the fourteenth-century and Tudor lodgings certainly were and are. At the back of the present south range, immediately adjacent to the Bell Tower, there is still preserved and visible an embrasure and loop of Longchamp's section of the south curtain, and there is the crumbling remains of another further east in the fourteenth-century basement. The west wing, which had no original predecessor, also masks some of the embrasures and loops of the shooting gallery in the west curtain, four of which can still be seen in that part of the basement called the 'Cow Shed'. One of the embrasures is now blocked but the other three are of early brick with stone quoins. Here also, excavations some years ago revealed the immense thickness of the foundations of the curtain wall itself.

Adjacent to the Queen's House to the north, and thus on the west side of Tower Green, stand two handsome seventeenth-century brick houses (Nos. 4 and 5 Tower Green), each of three storeys with attics and basement. They too, are built against the west curtain and mask six of its original embrasures and loops. Again, those of the embrasures which can be seen are of early brick with stone quoins. The whole of the wall-walk or parapet along the curtain between the Bell and Beauchamp towers (with access from each) survives, though restored, and is known as Elizabeth's Walk.

The **Chapel of St Peter-ad-Vincula** stands on the north side of Tower Green and in the north-west corner of the main inner bailey. In its present form it is a small Tudor church (of which there are not many to be seen) rebuilt in *c* 1519–20 after a fire in 1512, and heavily restored in 1876–77, when the south porch shown on the 1597 plan (Pl VII) was removed, the west tower rebuilt, and the present vestry added to the north-east. In origin, as stated above (p 20), it is merely a parish church of the city, taken into the castle by the great extension in this area by Henry III, and subsequently rebuilt by Edward I. Inside, the church consists of nave and chancel without any architectural division, and an arcaded north aisle as wide as the nave itself, both with flat tie-beam roofs. Older work is said to be contained in the north wall, and the crypt, now almost entirely refaced with eighteenth-century and later brick, lies to the north of the church, leading to the suggestion that it may possibly mark one of the earlier structures. There are three tombs of particular artistic note. The oldest, in the north-west corner of the chapel, is that of John Holland, Duke of Exeter (1395–1447), canopied and with effigies of himself and his first and third wives, respectively Anne of Stafford and Anne of Salisbury. This monument does not properly belong here but stood originally in the chapel of St Katherine's Hospital near the Tower, whence it was moved with that foundation to Regent's Park in 1827 and finally to its present position in 1951. The alabaster altar-tomb, with effigies, of Sir Richard Cholmoundeley (1544) and Elizabeth his wife, stands in the north aisle.

The Elizabethan memorials to the Blounts, father and son, and both Lieutenants, stand on the north wall of the chancel.

The principal interest of the Chapel of St Peter-ad-Vincula, however, lies neither in its funeral monuments nor in its architecture but in its associations. Here were buried, beneath the chancel, without ceremony, dignity or even memorial, many of those executed in the Tudor period on Tower Green outside, a place of death reserved for those most distinguished whose public execution on Tower Hill might in any case cause trouble. They include three queens, Anne Boleyn, Katherine Howard and the uncrowned Lady Jane Grey. Their ultimate justice may be that they are now amongst the best remembered historical personages in the realm. During the restoration of the 1870s their pathetic remains, in so far as they could be recovered, were treated with all possible respect at the special request of Queen Victoria, and reburied with a suitable memorial. Pray for them, and perhaps those who slew them, who doubtless need our prayers more.

To the east of the chapel and occupying almost the whole of the north side of the inner bailey is the solid, castellated, mid-nineteenth century mass of the **Waterloo Block** (formerly barracks), built under the auspices of the Duke of Wellington as Constable to accommodate nearly 1000 soldiers, after fire in 1841 had destroyed the late seventeenth-century Grand Storehouse of the Ordnance Office which formerly stood on this site. The pediment from the Grand Storehouse, which is all that remains of it, is now housed within the New Armouries (below). Next to the Waterloo Block, dating from the same period and the first of the line of buildings down the east side of the inner bailey, is the former Officers'

Mess and now the museum of the Royal Fusiliers. There follow two handsome eighteenth-century houses (the northern restored after bomb damage in the last war), now used as official residencies but formerly the Hospital Block, and next to them stands another handsome building dating from the late seventeenth century. This is the New Armouries, formerly the Horse Armoury, built in 1663–64 in the reign of Charles II.

More or less opposite the New Armouries and close to the south-east apsidal projection of the White Tower stands the **Wardrobe Tower** (Pl IV). Now in ruins, this is generally attributed to Longchamp in the 1190s, though may just possibly date from Henry II's time, in which case it is the oldest mural tower in the castle (pp 14–15 above). D-shaped in plan, it stands upon the line of the Roman city wall, which formed the eastern curtain of the Tower until the 1230s (p 20 above) and is hereabouts marked in the grass, and it contains in its base and foundations the visible remains of a Roman bastion whose site it occupies. It is clearly shown on the 1597 plan (Pl VII) and there called the Wardrobe Tower, though depicted as cylindrical (with a cylindrical turret). From it in 1597 the Wardrobe building ran east to the Broad Arrow Tower, and it is clear that by the late medieval period the whole area south of this line had been developed into a further and subsidiary palace ward or courtyard, bounded by the wardrobe to the north, the King's Lodgings on the west, the King's Gallery on the south, and the inner curtain from the Broad Arrow Tower to the Salt Tower on the east. The palace buildings had thus expanded into the two-court plan fashionable in late medieval great houses, and to the south of this second court, on the other side of the King's Gallery,

A. West Curtain Wall

lay the Privy Garden and the private, royal watergate of Edward III's Cradle Tower (p 81 above). All this has now gone, save only the Cradle, Salt and Broad Arrow towers, to be described below, and the site of the palace is now grass. Here the new **History Gallery**, illustrating the history of the Tower, has recently been built and opened, and close to it lies the surviving section of the fourth-century Roman city wall (p 5 above), revealed in the attendant excavations.

It remains only to describe the inner and outer curtains of the castle (Figs 1, 15 and 16), and the towers which stand upon them in so far as these have not been described already. The inner is, of course, much the more formidable of the two, the outer curtain being originally a low revetment wall on the three landward sides, adequately covered by the main defences behind it which required a clear field of fire. A section of the great inner curtain from the Wakefield to the Martin Tower is now open to the public, affording not only agreeable prospects in most directions from the wall-walk itself but also an inspection of those parts of the mural towers through which one passes. Of these, Lanthorn and Constable are nineteenth-century rebuildings but Wakefield (p 53 above), Salt, Broad

FIGURE 16 *Curtain Wall Elevations:* A *Inner South Curtain from Bell Tower to Salt Tower;* B *Outer South Curtain from Byward Tower to Develin Tower*

B. Section through Flint Tower to St Thomas's Tower

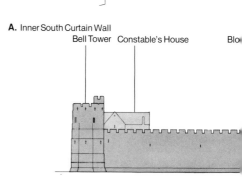

A. Inner South Curtain Wall

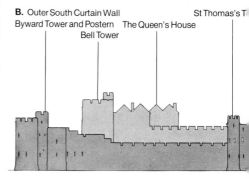

B. Outer South Curtain Wall

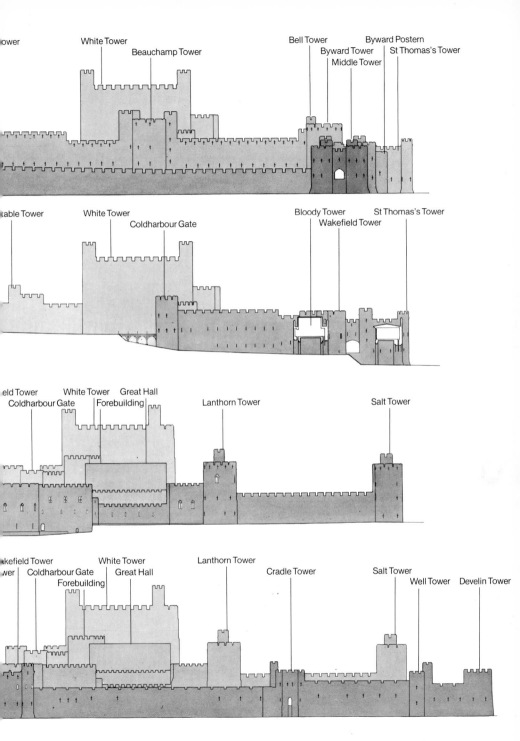

ower
White Tower
Beauchamp Tower
Bell Tower
Byward Postern
Byward Tower
St Thomas's Tower
Middle Tower

able Tower
White Tower
Coldharbour Gate
Bloody Tower
Wakefield Tower
St Thomas's Tower

eld Tower
White Tower
Great Hall
Coldharbour Gate
Forebuilding
Lanthorn Tower
Salt Tower

akefield Tower
wer
Coldharbour Gate
Forebuilding
White Tower
Great Hall
Lanthorn Tower
Cradle Tower
Salt Tower
Well Tower
Develin Tower

Arrow and Martin are originals albeit altered, and they make one message very plain—that mural towers though an integral part of a castle's defences, and strong-points providing flanking fire, were also residential, with chambers for kings and princes, courtiers and officials. The castle as a whole, and therefore in its parts, was the fortified residence of its lord and his household, a residential fortress in a society predominantly military in its upper reaches.

With the exception of modern restorations and even rebuildings, the whole of the **inner curtain** dates from Henry III's time (pp 17–22 above), save for the western side which, with the Beauchamp Tower in the midst of it, was built by Edward I (p 23 above), and for the section of the south wall from the Bell Tower inclusive to the Bloody Tower exclusive, which is the work of Longchamp in the 1190s (p 15 above). Along the south (Fig 16), the Bell Tower (p 44), the Bloody Tower (p 49) and the Wakefield Tower (p 53) have been described already. Next came the **Lanthorn Tower**, so called on the 1597 plan but not in the beginning, destroyed by fire in 1774, demolished in 1777 and entirely rebuilt in the late nineteenth century on a slightly different site. Of no architectural interest now, therefore, it has certain nineteenth-century exhibits for the visitor who passes through at first-floor level via two new forced openings from and to the wall-walk. The original Lanthorn was built at the same time as the Wakefield in the 1220s and 1230s together with the curtain between them (now also mainly a late nineteenth-century reconstruction), and though it is smaller in scale than the latter both are exceptional among the mural towers of Henry III's curtain in size and cylindrical shape. The Wakefield in Henry III's day was a veritable *donjon circulaire* with the king's

privy chamber within it, and the Lanthorn, too, in the fourteenth and fifteenth centuries had the distinction of royal residence, with a chamber block beside it on the west (pp 29, 33 above).

The curtain wall from the Lanthorn to the south-east angle is again a late nineteenth-century rebuild, but the **Salt Tower** survives, albeit thoroughly restored in the nineteenth century, as one of the original angle towers of Henry III. It probably belongs to the next and main phase of his curtain which began in *c* 1238 (p 20 above), and may be early as it, too, is more completely cylindrical than the others (i.e. Martin and Devereux) though rather smaller in scale. A boldly projecting three-quarters of a cylinder externally, it has a rectangular staircase turret to the north, incorporated in the east curtain to rise above roof level, and a smaller, rectangular projection to the west giving access to the wall-walk of the south curtain. Projecting from its external face, and necessarily additions of Edward I's reign, are the remains of two of the cross walls which formerly barred the outer bailey, one south to the Well Tower and one east to the eastern curtain. As built, the tower had a basement and two residential floors but now has an inserted third floor. Though now entered by the visitor from the wall-walk through a reopened original doorway, the ground-floor entrance from the inner bailey is through a short mural passage and a restored doorway into the north-west corner of the basement. This is an irregular pentagon in shape, with a timber ceiling and five splayed loops within embrasures with rather flat two-centred arches. An original doorway, north and next to the entrance, leads to the vice in the staircase turret, from which, at this level and north again, there is access via a square-headed doorway and steps up into a small mural chamber in the east curtain. This was probably in origin one of the line of embrasures for loops here, but now has on the left or west a doorway out into the bailey (above ground level and visible from outside) where there must have been some annexe or building now vanished. The **first floor** through which the visitor passes is again an irregular pentagon in shape and contains what has been a very nice chamber, with a grand original and hooded fireplace in the south wall opposite the entrance, and access to an original garderobe a few steps up the vice. On the right of the fireplace, facing west and outside the curtain, there is a fine but rebuilt window of two trefoil lights with a quatrefoil above and between. Right of this again is the restored doorway leading from the wall-walk of the south curtain. On the other side of the room, north, east and south-east, there are three loops, splayed and two-centred with similar reveals. On the way up the vice to the second floor, at the same level as the garderobe, there is a doorway giving on to the wall-walk of the east curtain, and now therefore the exit from the tower. The second floor is of the same shape as that below and was originally of much the same plan but is now more restored and altered. The timber ceiling is obviously too low, indicating that the floor above is an insertion, and the south wall opposite the entrance is blank where an original fireplace probably stood. To the right of this there is a semi-original lancet and a rebuilt two-light window of the same pattern as the one below but this time in the western projection of the tower above the wall-walk. To the left or east there are three much restored splayed loops which were probably lancets originally at this level. The present third floor seems entirely an insertion, marrying with the

considerable modern restoration and rebuilding of the top of the tower, and contains no features of interest. The vice continues to the modern roof and parapet. The Salt Tower contains many inscriptions, almost all of sixteenth-century date and on the first floor.

The east curtain running north from the Salt Tower to Broad Arrow is in part original and contained at least two cruciform loops with the embrasures behind them now hidden by the Armoury buildings. Immediately south of Broad Arrow and integral with the structure of the tower there is a broad and handsome original postern (Fig 9A and B, Pl XXIV), with a segmental-pointed arch of two orders, piercing the wall. Hidden now from the inside by the Armouries, it is visible from the outside where it opens several feet above the ground. It is clear that the northerly rising ground in this area has been dug away subsequently, thus exposing too much of the base of both curtain and towers.

The **Broad Arrow Tower** itself (so-called in 1597) is of considerable interest as a comparatively unaltered mural tower of Henry III's works after *c* 1238 (Figs 2, 9A and B, Pl XXIV). D-shaped externally, its inner face is flush with the curtain and has two rectangular turrets respectively north and south, the northern containing the staircase and the southern solid up to first-floor level to accommodate the postern. Originally it was of two floors only and is still so described by Clark in 1884, the present top floor therefore being a late nineteenth-century insertion. On the 1597 plan (Pl VII) the Wardrobe Building abuts it and no doubt had come to incorporate it. It is now entered at first-floor level by the visitor from the wall-walk but its ground-level entrance from the bailey is via a narrow alley north of the New Armouries through a restored two-centred doorway. The ground-floor room is more or less rectangular with a timbered ceiling, and had three loops with pointed embrasures. The eastern embrasure is now fitted with a modern two-light trefoil window, but those north and south still have cruciform loops and the former is at a higher level to accommodate the ground level rising to the north. In the west wall, next to the entrance, there is a restored window of one trefoil light, and on the other side of the entrance, in the north wall, an original doorway with a shouldered arch leads to the stairway constructed in the thickness of the curtain and ascending the northern turret. The stairway is not spiral but straight and dog-legged, and on the landing there is a restored window to the west and a blocked loop to the east. The **first floor**, the same shape as that below, was clearly the best and residential chamber. This is the apartment seen by visitors passing through from the wall-walk south to north, and is furnished as it might have been in the late fourteenth century, more precisely in 1381 and in the time of Sir Simon Burley, KG, whose coat armour and arms are displayed. There is a hooded but totally renewed fireplace and a garderobe which is situated off the pointed-arched mural passage running from the entrance from the wall-walk to the south into the chamber. There are three loops with embrasures, north, east and south, as on the floor below, but that on the east is skewed to avoid the fireplace while that on the south is much restored. In the west wall there is a large two-light trefoil window which is a nineteenth-century insertion. As in the Salt Tower, it is clear that the present timber ceiling of the room is too low as the result of the modern

PLATE XXIV *The Broad Arrow and postern. Note the line of the original ground level descending to the river*

insertion of the floor above. Exit to the wall-walk to the north is by a stairway six steps up, again to accommodate the rising ground and the consequent higher section of the curtain north of the tower. The inserted top floor forms a thoroughly disagreeable room, mostly faced with crude brickwork of eighteenth-century date or later, but has a Victorian two-light window in the west wall, of the same pattern as the one below it. The stairway in the northern turret, above the level of the exit to the wall-walk, becomes a vice to reach this top floor, and so continues to the roof. The Broad Arrow Tower contains many inscriptions on both its original floors, again evidently dating from the sixteenth and seventeenth centuries.

Next in line to the north after Broad Arrow comes the **Constable Tower** (Fig 1) of the same D-shaped plan but almost entirely a nineteenth-century rebuilding. The curtain wall to the south of it is partly original, but that to the north has been entirely rebuilt or refaced and the base of this whole section is exposed by the levelling of the rising ground in this area as noted above (houses stood here until the late nineteenth century).

Next, and standing at the north-east angle of Henry III's curtain, comes the **Martin Tower** (Fig 1). Recently repaired, it exhibits many features, especially internally, which are unusual in that they reflect the developments in the Tower in the seventeenth and eighteenth centuries. Basically D-shaped in plan, it projects very boldly to the field, as befits an angle tower, and is then, so to speak, squared-off on its southern and western sides, with two rectangular turrets on and in the west and north curtains respectively. Externally the tower is much refaced with later brickwork and has also many 'classical' and eighteenth-century features especially on the west and south sides. Thus it has an incongruous front door of c 1725 with a wooden hood at first-floor level reached by a modern staircase, and another door of similar date with a triangular pediment giving on to the wall-walk to the south from which the visitor now enters. Above this there is a presumably contemporary sundial set in the south wall, and elsewhere there are sash windows. All this, together with later eighteenth-century alterations, partitions and panelling within, are the remaining signs of its occupation by the Keeper of the Crown Jewels until the mid-nineteenth century. Later and until recently it was occupied by the military and thus escaped the thorough-going restorations of Salvin in the mid-nineteenth century, so that it still retains much original work, however masked. There were originally only two storeys and the entrance from the bailey at ground-floor level is still there, though altered and widened, beneath an arch carrying the altered early eighteenth-century stairs to the front door. Within is a kind of entrance lobby contrived in the thickness of the east curtain, with, immediately on the left or north, a good, original, pointed-arched doorway, rebated on the inside, leading via a skewed passage to a garderobe in the north turret. This has had a doorway hacked through its south wall back into the bailey (and now blocked again), presumably to make it a cell at some late period when the tower served as a prison. Opposite the garderobe doorway in the entrance lobby there is an altered late-medieval doorway, still revealing some traces of the original and leading to the vice in the south turret. Here, again, a way has been forced at a late date from the foot of the stairway into the adjacent (southern) embrasure of the main ground-floor room, presumably to make of it a cell or a porter's lodge. The main ground-floor room is an irregular hexagon in shape and had a timbered ceiling, five embrasures with loops, and a once splendid fireplace in the south-east wall. Of the embrasures, two (north-east and west) have recently been restored with loops to their original appearance, two (north and east) have nineteenth-century two-light windows in them, and the south embrasure (cut into from the vice) has an eighteenth-century sash-window. The **first floor** was reached via the vice in the south turret, either up from the ground floor (past a small window on the right revealing traces of an original loop), or down from the wall-walk with the modern visitor, and so into the western embrasure of the main chamber through an altered and widened doorway in its south wall. This embrasure has a rear arch with a hollow moulding, which is a rare feature in the Tower of London (cf St Thomas's Tower and the Cradle Tower), and is occupied by the *c* 1725 front door in the place of an original window, in front of which further steps from the vice curve up awkwardly. Opposite the entrance from the vice, in the north wall, an almost vanished pointed-arched doorway leads to a garderobe (its two-centred doorway recently restored), situated in the northern turret and above the corresponding garderobe on the ground floor, and a barrel-vaulted passage, running west with steps up, to the wall-walk of the northern curtain. In the south wall of this passage a later forced doorway, now blocked, led out of the turret. It must at least be earlier than the 1725 front door and may have been closed when that was inserted. The main chamber itself at this level was much like the ground floor chamber, with five embrasures for windows or loops and a formerly grand fireplace in the south-east wall. A mezzanine floor, however, with a staircase (by the west embrasure) and landing of the same date, was inserted above it in the late seventeenth century, reducing the proper height of the room and cutting across the heads of the embrasures. Of these, the south embrasure is still in a near-original state but the others have been hacked into wide window openings, the western now bricked up, the eastern with a nineteenth-century two-light window, and the northern and north-eastern fitted with 'Georgian' sash-windows and shutters. Above all these embrasures other wide openings have been cut to give light and air to the mezzanine floor, all of them save the eastern fitted with eighteenth-century sash-windows and panelling. The south staircase turret with its vice goes on up from the first floor to the roof, past two small windows which are former loops and the early eighteenth-century door from the eastern wall-walk between them. The vice no longer ascends beyond the main roof to the turret as it should, but both this turret and its northern neighbour have much original work right to their summits, which is an unusual phenomenon at the Tower. The Martin Tower has inscriptions at all levels, including two of greater antiquity than the usual sixteenth- and seventeenth-century inscriptions and one in Irish.

In the north inner curtain wall from Martin to Devereux (Fig 1) there is little externally that is visibly ancient, it having been at least refaced, and both the **Brick Tower** and the **Flint Tower** are nineteenth-century rebuildings (the former was still standing in 1825 but the latter was rebuilt from the foundations soon after 1800). The **Bowyer Tower** between them, however, though entirely refaced and its upper stage modern, still contains its original ground floor. It stands on the line of the Roman city wall which was revealed beneath its floor in 1911, and has recently been refurbished and made over to educational displays (if imprisonment and improbable post-medieval tortures may be so described). Two storeys high, it has a staircase turret on the east, no longer accessible to the public and now projecting into the bailey with a modern doorway into it. The tower is entered through a modern and widened doorway in place of the original in the south wall. The ground floor chamber is, or was, very handsome, and is vaulted with a simple quadripartite vault of a single chamfered order. The room, like the tower, is roughly D-shaped and has three embrasures for loops, respectively east, west and north. Only the western loop survives and the other two embrasures have modern two-light windows. Above the entrance there is a large blocked archway, possibly a window for some formerly inserted floor, and to the east of this, also in the south wall, is the doorway to the turret staircase, at the foot of which there was probably also a garderobe to complete the domestic amenities of the room. Next to this, inserted in the east wall, is a pair of very nice square-headed cupboards. In the west wall, south or left of the embrasure, there is an arched recess, now blocked with brick, the remains of a former fireplace.

The **Devereux Tower** (Figs 1 and 15) standing at the north-west corner of the inner bailey is (with the exception of the special case of the Wakefield above) the most massive of Henry III's angle towers, doubtless because it faced the city. Indeed it is very evident that all three towers on the western curtain, Devereux, Beauchamp and Bell, though of varying dates, are of abnormal strength, as is the curtain itself with its formidable shooting gallery. The Devereux Tower is called Develin on the 1597 plan, and earlier in the sixteenth century was Robert the Devil's Tower (i.e. Robert, duke of Normandy and father of William the Conqueror). It is now the residence of a yeoman warder and not open to the public. It stands within a courtyard which is raised above the proper ground level to obscure the base of the tower on that side and which is entered through a handsome but unrecorded late medieval screen wall with a series of buttresses on its east face and two archways. The tower is a very irregular D-shape in plan and stood two storeys high with one staircase turret on the south-east which led from the ground floor to the upper floor and roof. A further stair turret to the south-west led only from the west wall-walk to the roof. The whole has been entirely refaced in the modern period, and the south front is much 'Georgianized' with sash windows and two inserted doors, one above the other, the upper reached by a modern external staircase. There is also a modern window on to the wall-walk of the west curtain. The original entrance on this south front and into the ground floor survives, but is now beneath the raised courtyard at what has thus become basement level. In front of it, extending south and also below the courtyard, is a vaulted brick casemate, within which two of the embrasures of the west curtain can be seen. They, like all these embrasures which can be seen, are of early brick (i.e. earlier than the brick of the casemate itself) with stone quoins. In the vault of the casemate there are two vents which may be smoke-vents similar to those found in artillery casemates but which here were more probably used in connection with industrial activity. The entrance into the tower itself is through an original doorway, rebated for a door on the inside, and so into the original ground floor. This formed a handsome chamber, vaulted like the ground floor of the Bowyer, and with a vault of similar fashion. The irregular shape of the room produces two bays, the first on entry quadripartite, the next tripartite, each of a single chamfered order. As in the Bowyer Tower again, there was also a fireplace at this level, now represented by a modern but ashlar reproduction in the south-west wall. Immediately right or east of the entrance doorway there is another original doorway, with an external rebate, leading to the vice up which at mezzanine level there is a garderobe, serving the ground floor. It is constructed in the thickness of the north curtain, and has been widened to the north but still has the remains of an original window to the south. The ground-floor room itself has three embrasures for loops, north, north-east and south-west, which have round heads like

PLATE XXV *An 1821 engraving of the first-floor chamber of the Beauchamp Tower, looking south*

those in the ground floor of the Wakefield. The northern still has a (restored) loop, and the other two are fitted with modern windows. The present first floor above the vault had a small modern fireplace to the southwest, marking the position of an original, and Bayley in 1825 refers to what sounds like a garderobe for the original first floor in the thickness of the north curtain like the one below it; recent work has confirmed this. This floor has the remains of three loops corresponding to those on the ground floor. Access from the west wall-walk entered the western vice just above first-floor level; the north wall-walk was reached from above first-floor level from the eastern vice. The upper part of the tower was modified in 1683, as a gun platform and again in 1715, when the present second floor was inserted.

The western inner curtain from Devereux to the Bell Tower via the Beauchamp Tower (Fig. 15) is one of the most formidable features of the castle, by reason of the three great flanking towers themselves and by reason of the continuous line of embrasures and loops along its whole length between them to form a shooting gallery towards the city (cf the Main Guard wall, p 59 above). It was built by Edward I in two vertical phases between 1275 and *c* 1281 to replace Henry III's curtain, and the Beauchamp Tower inserted in the middle of it about the latter year to replace Henry's gate-tower on the same site (above p 23). The loops of the gallery are 3.5m apart and also 3.5m above the present ground level of the outer ward, which is evidence that the outer curtain beyond was originally much lower than it is now. In all observed cases the embrasures of the loops are constructed of ancient brick with stone quoins. There is no obvious sign that this brickwork is a later facing or adaptation, and in view of the amount of brick-work still visible within the Beauchamp Tower (below), and of a section of again ancient brick-work still visible on the inner face of the curtain immediately south of that tower, there can be little doubt that these bricks are original, i.e. of the time of Edward I—who, it will be recalled, sold off quantities of earth from his new ditch about the Tower, including clay to the London 'tilers' (p 22 above).

The **Beauchamp Tower** (Pl viii, Figs 1 and 15) was thus built in c 1281 by Edward I. A majestic D-shaped tower of unusual span to cover the former entrance (which was doubtless a twin-towered gatehouse), and its inner face flush with the curtain, it stands three storeys high, topped by rectangular turrets to north and south. Refaced externally, it is full of interest within, and very obviously contained particularly grand residential accommodation (which later made it especially suitable for the confinement of important political prisoners in the Tudor period). It is entered from the bailey at ground-floor level through a doorway on the left or south side of its east wall. On the left as one enters is a passage to the vice which ascends the southern turret. The ground floor chamber itself is now used for storage and closed to visitors. It was a handsome apartment, very lofty but with a timbered ceiling, rectangular in shape but bowed out to the west within the projecting semi-circle which the tower presents to the field. There are five embrasures in the projection—north, west and south, plus south-west and north-west—each with pointed arches of brick. Four of these still have cross-loops in them, but the south-

west embrasure has a fireplace, basically ashlar but with a brick inset and no surviving hood, probably nineteenth-century in date. In the east wall of the room, i.e. facing Tower Green, there is a large nineteenth-century two-light window. Nearby, in the right-hand side of the north wall and opposite the doorway to the vice, a similar, two-centred doorway leads into a passage in the northern turret of the tower, with a loop on the left and a garderobe at its end, also on the left and also with a loop. Opposite the garderobe and opposite the first loop there is a small window on to the bailey. Throughout this ground-floor level, not only in the arches of the embrasures as already noted but also in the walls, the vice and the turret passage, the extensive use of contemporary brick is very noticeable. It appears also in the upper levels of the tower though there less visible because of modern plaster, paint and other decorations (the exterior, of course, has been entirely refaced). The first-floor chamber, which is open to visitors, is entered from the vice through a pointed-arched doorway. In plan it is similar to the room below but is less lofty. Again there are five embrasures with pointed arches in positions corresponding to those below, four with cross-loops and the south-westerly with an original fireplace, square-headed and now lacking a hood. The east wall again has a large nineteenth-century two-light window looking on to Tower Green and the White Tower, and next to this, in the north wall, is a pointed-arched doorway into the north turret and a passage (in good condition and still with its pointed barrel-vault) leading to the garderobe, with loops and opposed windows as on the floor below. Here again brick is very evident but at this level the passage ends at a blocked original doorway formerly opening on to the wall-walk of the curtain. The entrance to the wall-walk to the south is off the vice in the south turret and a little higher up. The vice leads on up to the roof via the second floor which is now divided up and converted into the official residence of a Yeoman Warder and in consequence is private and shows no original features. Here there is a two-light window facing west in place of the loops below, and there is also a room in the top of the northern turret, which in fact is larger (in extending further to the north) than its southern counterpart. The Beauchamp Tower contains many inscriptions not all of which belong here.

Though now much heightened, and masked by buildings which abut against it, the **outer curtain** as built by Edward I (p 22 above) must have been a low revetment wall to be cleared by the missiles of the main defences of the inner curtain behind it (cf Beaumaris). The long line of loops in the western inner curtain are thus only 3.5m above the present ground level of the outer ward. While on the three landward sides it is by no means certain how long these arrangements lasted, the wall along the river front is known to have been heightened as early as the first half of the fourteenth century and here certainlythere were towers from the beginning, all save one of them the work of Edward I.

Of the towers along the south outer curtain (Fig 16), the Byward gate-tower with its adjacent postern, and St Thomas's water-gate (now the Traitors' Gate) have been described already (pp 38, 47 above). Next to the east, after a modern gateway, comes the **Cradle Tower** (Fig 17 and Pl XI), built by Edward III between 1348 and 1355 as a new and privy water-gate to the royal apartments by then in and adjacent to the Lanthorn Tower. By the early nineteenth

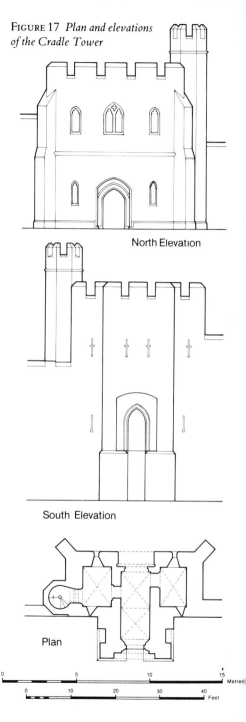

FIGURE 17 *Plan and elevations of the Cradle Tower*

North Elevation

South Elevation

Plan

century it is known that the Cradle Tower had been cut down to make a gun platform, so that when Bayley described it in 1825 only the lower part was extant and the whole of the top hamper and upper floor is now a nineteenth-century rebuilding. The lower levels, however, comprising the two gateways and the gate passage between them with two lobbies respectively on either side, east and west, are still for the most part in their original regal and sophisticated condition. Much smaller than the state watergate of St Thomas's, the Cradle Tower is T-shaped in plan with the stem projecting into what was the river and containing the entrance therefrom. This projection stands over two half-arches for the passage of the water, and on either side, east and west, are arched recesses of differing width, with an original garderobe shaft from the upper floor hidden in the thickness of the wall north of the east recess. The entrance from the river on the south front is within a wide recess with a flat segmental head, and is itself of two moulded orders, the outer hollow and the inner boldly rounded, with a pointed, two-centred arch. On either side the grooves for a portcullis are clearly visible from the Wharf, from which this view is obtained. The portal is now closed by a modern timber grill but retains a massive iron hinge on the east side and two drawbar holes on the west. The rear arch is two-centred and segmental with a recessed ovolo or flattened roll moulding. Within there was evidently a drawbridge, and, presumably, a jetty without. The entrance passage is handsomely vaulted in two bays (Pl XI). The vault is chalk and the ribs Reigate, meeting in a hollow circle in each bay and springing from three pairs of corbels of which the southernmost pair are grotesque animals characteristically mid fourteenth-

century in type. On either side of the entrance passage towards its north end there is a doorway. That on the east is close to the north gateway and original albeit restored. It leads into a small rectangular and vaulted room which must have been a porter's lodge and is now heavily modified. There is a damaged and recently discovered fireplace in the east wall, of fourteenth-century date, square-headed and with a contemporary or near-contemporary bread-oven in its south-east corner. The single-light window with a cinquefoil head in the north wall looking into the outer bailey is more or less original, but the smaller window in the south wall towards the river is restored. The ribs of the quadripartite vault spring from enriched corbels. The doorway off the entrance passage on the west side has been moved and rebuilt: it was originally further south and not opposite its eastern fellow. This at once suggests some different function from that of another porter's lodge for the room or lobby to which it gives access, and which in all probability was an outer entrance vestibule to the royal apartments, reached from here by a vice and a bridge (now vanished but cf St Thomas's Tower) across the outer bailey. This vice, though now itself rebuilt and leading to the rebuilt upper floor, is really an adjunct to the tower built partly in the outer curtain to the west, and is gained by a wide and rather grand original doorway through the west wall of the vestibule. For the rest, the vestibule is similar in design to the porter's lodge on the other side of the tower (though without a fireplace), with a similar and original north window, a rebuilt and smaller south window, and a quadripartite vault springing from corbels of which the north-eastern still exhibits a small animal grotesque. The rear-arch of the northern gateway from the entrance passage to the inner ward is similar in form to that of the southern, river gateway, but is, so to speak, reversed in its moulding, having a hollow chamfer with beaded edges. The north front of the Cradle Tower facing the outer ward is again impressive in its lower and original level, with the tall lancet windows of the lobbies, each with a cinquefoil head, one on either side of the elaborate entrance. The latter has, first, the pointed and two-centred arch of the gateway itself, with a boldly rounded chamfered order slightly recessed on the face; next, the portcullis groove; and then an outer arch of two main orders (the inner a boldly rounded and slightly recessed chamfer, the outer a recessed and rounded moulding with a hollow chamfer) both dying into the hollow-moulded jambs.

The **Well Tower** (Figs 1 and 16) stands to the east of the Cradle as a mural tower of Edward I upon his new south outer curtain and thus belongs to the works of 1275–85 (pp 22–27 above). A rectangular tower two storeys high with a rectangular staircase turret at the north-east, it projects slightly into the outer ward and much more deeply to the river. Not the least of its interests is the cross-wall integral with it and running north from its north-west angle to the Salt Tower opposite to bar the inner ward (Fig 1). Surviving in part to wall-walk height, enough of this remains to show something of the original arrangements, with the parapet facing east and the wall-walk gained from a doorway at first-floor level in the Well Tower. The springing of the archway of the gate through the wall can just be seen, and south of this are two embrasures with loops, again facing east and evidently original. Much less of the companion cross-wall running east from the Salt Tower survives, but it had the same

profile, with its parapet and loops facing south. The Well Tower is entered at ground-floor level through a partly restored, pointed-arched doorway in the west wall, masked by a modern lobby. The ground-floor chamber is vaulted in two quadripartite bays, the ribs springing from differing corbels two of which have two deeply undercut moulded orders. In the south wall are two recently revealed shoots evidently for drawing water from the river, which make the name of this tower more meaningful than most and perhaps even original. Above and between them there is a restored, splayed cross-loop. Similar loops in the east and west covered the outer face of the curtain, and in the west wall, below the loop, there is a drain-hole which may mark the original floor level as a little higher than now. In the north wall there is the curious arrangement of another similar loop (covering the outer face of the cross-wall barring the bailey) with a restored single-light window above it and a fireplace below to the right and intruding upon it. The latter is certainly not contemporary and may be altogether a modern insertion since this tower has no garderobes to indicate an original residential function. Near the fireplace but in the east wall, a tall, square-headed and chamfered doorway, later or altered in its present form, leads to the vice in the staircase turret, which ascends via recessed cross-loops south, east and north to the first floor and the roof. Bayley in 1825 found only the lower part of the Well Tower to be original with its upper floor then a 'modern dwelling', and the upper stages now are evidently a nineteenth-century restoration and partial rebuilding, incorporating ancient features where possible. Thus the first-floor room is entered down two steps from the vice through a doorway with an original pointed

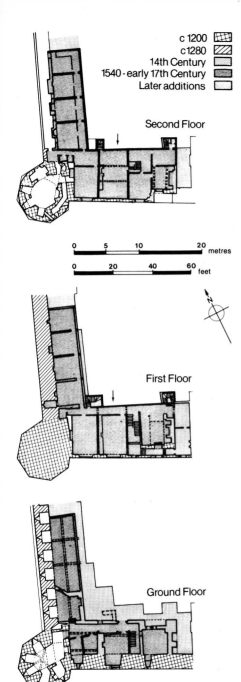

FIGURE 18 *Floor plans of the Queen's House*

rear-arch at the north end of the east wall, and the doorway on the north side of the room to the wall-walk of the cross-wall is similarly original inside though heavily restored without. The fireplace, in a position corresponding to that on the floor below but smaller, is again an insertion. The present square-headed, two-light window in the west wall is Victorian but the splayed loops in the south and east walls, with their oddly shaped heads are at least in part original. There are inscriptions of sixteenth and seventeenth-century date at this level of the tower.

The **Develin Tower** (Fig 1), named simply as 'The Tower leading to the Iron Gate' on the 1597 plan (Pl vii), was partly rebuilt in 1679 and later has served as a powder magazine. It is, and evidently was, a two-storeyed structure entirely projecting into the eastern arm of the moat, with its south side thus appearing as a continuation of the south outer curtain. Its only present features of interest are themselves post-medieval, namely a blocked late seventeenth-century doorway at first-floor level in the east wall, and a restored early Tudor casemate adjacent to its north-west corner at ground-floor level, angled to rake the moat. In its original form it was a postern tower with the passageway running through it and connected by a walled causeway with the Iron Gate beyond (now vanished).

Brass Mount and Legge's Mount (Fig 1), respectively at the north-east and north-west angles of the outer curtain, are in their present form semi-circular bastions added for defence by guns. Both have been much altered so that their original arrangements are not easy to determine. In the case of the Brass Mount, excavations in 1913 revealed the line of Edward I's wall running through and behind, forming an obtuse

PLATE XXVI *Aerial photograph of the Tower of London from the south in July 1980, with HM Yacht Britannia entering the Pool of London*

angle in the curtain. Both were stone structures rising through two stages with parapets, and both were originally open, but otherwise they are not the same, the Brass Mount being larger and with a greater projection. While both bastions are usually attributed to Henry VIII, Legge's Mount is undoubtedly earlier, for recent work has shown that its lower part is contemporary with Edward I's curtain, and the basement has an inserted skin and vault of early Tudor brick. This bastion was converted into Yeomen Warders' lodgings in 1853 and before that had for centuries been made over to the Mint, and thereafter the Ordnance, which accounts for the brick hearths in what is now its northern division. The subsequent crosswall dividing the bastion and its heightening to provide the gunports visible in its upper part all date from the seventeenth century. A bomb-proof vault inserted in the early nineteenth century is one of the more interesting pieces of evidence for military defence at this late period. Brass Mount still serves as a modern armoury, and both its present floors above the basement are insertions. The outer wall, however, is basically original within though partly refaced externally, and is pierced by a mural gallery entered at present first-floor level. This is lined with early brick, its embrasures adapted for guns. Other traces of earlier arrangements survive including an evidently original embrasure, east north-east, with an outward splay and fitted with an eighteenth-century iron grill shaped for a gun. At the south end of this gallery there was originally a group of three garderobes, whose shoots remain, and there was another similar group at the other, north-western, end. Due south of Brass Mount there were three small towers with solid stone batters projecting and descending into the moat, which recent excavations have shown to be medieval in date. Two of the towers have now vanished and all three batters are hidden by the infilling of the moat, but the third tower, furthest from Brass Mount, still survives though largely refaced in the modern period. The purpose of these structures is uncertain, but they may have been for the mounting of stone-throwing engines, as much used in the medieval period for the defence of castles as were later cannon. More or less centrally between Brass Mount and Legge's Mount, at the salient in the north outer curtain, another bastion was added as late as 1848 at the time of the Chartist riots. This was demolished by a German bomb on 5 October, 1940, and has not been rebuilt.

Tower Hill Postern

On the north side of Edward I's moat, outside the Tower of London and on the line of the Roman city wall, stand the excavated remains of the medieval city gate known as the Tower Hill Postern (Fig 19). Its preservation is due to the fact that its proximity to the ditch of the Tower of London caused it to subside over six feet,

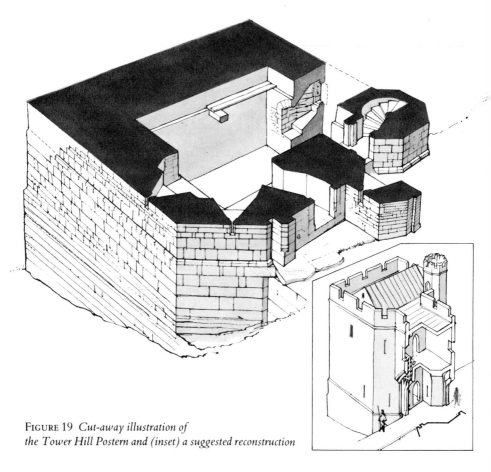

FIGURE 19 *Cut-away illustration of the Tower Hill Postern and (inset) a suggested reconstruction*

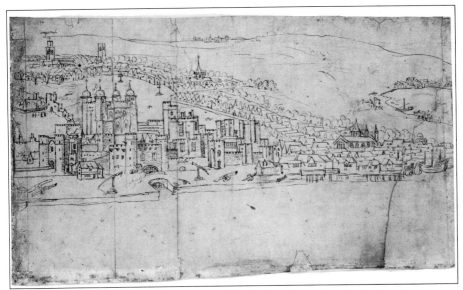

PLATE XXVII *Wyngaerde's panoramic drawing showing the Tower of London in the mid-sixteenth century*

effectively burying it. It is tempting to equate this subsidence with that mentioned by Stowe in his Survey of London who records it as taking place in 1440. He states that it was never rebuilt properly, only a timber superstructure being provided. The original which may have formed its sub-structure was, he tells us 'partly built of hard stone of Kent [i.e. Ragstone] and partly of stone brought from Caen in Normandy'. The postern's unexpected discovery in 1978 during the construction of a new road and subsequent excavation confirms Stowe's description, although there is some use of Purbeck marble—possibly re-used. A slight re-alignment of the road enabled the remains to be preserved.

The surviving part of the postern consists of the lower parts of the southernmost side of the gate-passage and the south gate-tower, the south wall of which must have immediately overlooked the moat of the Tower within comfortable bowshot of its outer curtain. Approximately twenty-five feet square in plan, the gate-tower is built of squared ragstone rubble with freestone dressings, a chamfered plinth at gate-passage level survives on the north and east faces, and a second lower offset exists on the east and south sides which faced the City ditch and the Tower moat. The north-east angle is chamfered and contains a loop which adjoins another loop at the north end of the east wall; these command the approach to the postern. The gate-passage was controlled by a portcullis set against the nicely stop-chamfered gate-jamb. Immediately to the west, a later doorway has been forced through the short length of wall before the gate-passage turns a dog-leg to the north. This short return, which sharply reduces the width of the entry passage, contains a loop facing forward and commanding the outer gate. This most unusual feature indicates that the passage was either narrowed or turned through two right-angles. Also unusual is the existence of a door jamb indicating that the gate-passage could be closed at its inner end by a gate opening eastwards. Since the north side at its presumed original higher level no longer survives, the exact form of the postern cannot be stated with any certainty but its form and designation as a postern suggests that it did not conform to the normal twin-towered gatehouse plan. A single tower overlooking the Tower of London moat, flanking a fairly narrow dog-legged entry, seems quite probable.

Beyond the crosswall an original doorway gave access to the ground floor of the tower and to a circular stair set in a semi-octagonal turret at the north-west angle.

The tower originally had three floors. The low basement survives, lit by a single upward splayed window in the west wall and probably approached by a ladder from the floor above which was of timber. The basement, apparently filled in during the sixteenth century, yielded numerous sections of chamfered vaulting ribs together with a hollowed-out roof boss. If these came from the tower they are likely to have been part of a first-floor vault with the form of the boss suggesting a fourteenth-century date. Original architectural enrichments to the ground floor survive in the form of the steep chamfers to the inner and outer gate-jambs

and the south jamb of the loop embrasure in the tower. These would be consistent with a thirteenth-century date. Documentary evidence shows the postern, which cannot be earlier than Edward I's construction of the moat and outer curtain to the Tower of London, to have been in existence by 1308.

Although the building and manning of the postern was clearly the responsibility of the City, the King's expansion of the Tower of London and resultant need of a new postern intimately connected with the Tower may have resulted in royal involvement in its construction. Certainly at a later period there was disagreement between the City and Tower authorities as to their jurisdiction over the postern which lay within the liberties of the Tower. The relationship with the Tower is underlined by the existence of two loops, now much altered, at a low level in the outer curtain of the Tower. These are placed exactly opposite the front and rear faces of the postern tower and would allow the Tower to command the postern.

The later history of the postern gate is not clear. Although Stowe clearly stated that it was never properly rebuilt, later maps of the Tower Hill area suggest that some sort of tower stood on the line of the city wall perhaps to the north.

The postern went out of use as a City gate in the early seventeenth century.

Glossary

ABACUS	Flat slab on capital, or uppermost part, of a column
APSIDAL	Semi-circular or polygonal in termination
ASHLAR	Hewn blocks of masonry laid in horizontal courses with fine vertical joints
AUMBRY	Recess in wall containing sacred vessels
BARREL-VAULTED	Uninterrupted vault (qv) of semi-circular section
BOSS	Ornamental projection at intersection of ribs (qv) or beams
CARTULARY	Register of records, especially charters
CENTERING	Temporary framing for an arch or vault during construction
CHAMFER	A flat, moulded or fluted bevel cut obliquely on a square-angled edge or corner
CORBEL	A projecting stone or piece of timber used as a support
CRENELLATION	Battlement or indented parapet, the openings of which are known as embrasures (qv)
CUPOLA	Small domed roof, often crowning a turret
DONJON	From Latin *dominium,* lordship; a keep, the strong-point of a Norman castle. *Donjon circulaire,* a round tower keep
EMBRASURE	Small opening in defensive wall or parapet, used as a shooting position
FLEUR DE LIS	Literally the flower of the lily; a floral ornament or heraldic decoration or carving; the royal arms of France
GARDEROBE	Privy or latrine, built usually in thickness of exterior wall and draining into moat or pit
JUSTICIAR	A chief administrator
LIGHT	Part of a glazed window, or opening for light. Subdivided further into panes. See also mullion and transom
LOOP	Narrow vertical slit in defensive wall, from which defenders shot bows and guns. Interior of loop was deeply splayed to increase the angle of fire
MEURTRIERE	A loop large enough for the barrel of a small gun or musket
MULLION	Vertical strut dividing window into lights (qv) and panes
MURDER HOLE	Aperture vertically above gateway, for its defence or to quench fire brought against it
OGEE	Arch of continuous double curve; convex and pointed above, and concave and bulbous below
PILASTER	Rectangular column projecting slightly from wall of building
PISCINA	Carved shallow basin, in which sacred vessels are washed

PORTAL	Especially elaborated doorway or entrance
PORTCULLIS	Heavy iron or wooden grating lowered vertically as defensive barrier at entrance of gatehouse
POSTERN	Small secondary entrance or gateway, often concealed and usually at rear of castle or military building
RAMPART	Protective stone or earth wall surrounding a fortress
REVETMENT	Retaining wall built to support or hold back a mass of earth or water
RIB	Projecting band of stone structurally supporting vault (qv) or purely decorative
RING-BEAM	Structural timber beam within wall of circular tower and supporting floor joists
ROMANESQUE	Style of architecture current in eleventh and twelfth centuries, characterized by round arches and vaults
SEDILIA	Series of seats, often recessed in wall and with canopies, on the south side of the chancel for use by clergy
STRING COURSE	A moulding or projecting band horizontally across the facade of a building or wall
TRANSOM	Horizontal strut dividing a window into lights (qv) and panes
TRIFORIUM	Arcaded wall passage, above and looking down on nave of church
VAULT	An arched roof or ceiling, usually supported decoratively by ribs (qv)
VICE	Spiral stair, with tapering steps around a central pillar or newel
VOLUTE	Carved stone scroll forming distinctive feature on capital, or uppermost part, of a column